AIR CAMPAIGN

ARCTIC CONVOYS 1942

The Luftwaffe cuts Russia's lifeline

MARK LARDAS | ILLUSTRATED BY ADAM TOOBY

OSPREY PUBLISHING
Bloomsbury Publishing Plc
Kemp House, Chawley Park, Cumnor Hill, Oxford OX2 9PH, UK
29 Earlsfort Terrace, Dublin 2, Ireland
1385 Broadway, 5th Floor, New York, NY 10018, USA
E-mail: info@ospreypublishing.com
www.ospreypublishing.com

OSPREY is a trademark of Osprey Publishing Ltd

First published in Great Britain in 2022

A catalog record for this book is available from the British Library.

ISBN: PB 9781472852434; eBook 9781472852441;
ePDF 9781472852410; XML 9781472852427

22 23 24 25 26 10 9 8 7 6 5 4 3 2 1

Maps by www.bounford.com
Diagrams by Adam Tooby
3D BEVs by Paul Kime
Index by Zoe Ross
Typeset by PDQ Digital Media Solutions, Bungay, UK
Printed and bound in India by Replika Press Private Ltd.

Osprey Publishing supports the Woodland Trust, the UK's leading woodland conservation charity.

To find out more about our authors and books visit www.ospreypublishing.com. Here you will find extracts, author interviews, details of forthcoming events and the option to sign up for our newsletter.

Author's note:
I would like to thank the RAF Museum and Darren Priday there for making available the image of the Handley Page Hampden P1344 used in the 'Surviving Aircraft' section.
The following abbreviations indicate the sources of the illustrations used in this volume:
AC – Author's Collection
LOC – Library of Congress
NMAF – National Museum of the Air Force
SDA&SM – San Diego Air & Space Museum
USNHHC – United States Navy Heritage and History Command

Author's dedication:
To the memory of LtC (ret) William Brendan Welsh, US Army Special Forces. I knew him as "Boss Mongo" on a message board, as good a friendship as I have ever had with someone I met only virtually. He admired my writing, while I admired his many accomplishments. We were going to meet up some day but never got the chance. You left us too soon, Boss.

CONTENTS

INTRODUCTION

By February 1942 the Allies had been running convoys to Russia via the Arctic route for six months. Losses had been light through to the end of that month and by then 97 ships had been sent to Murmansk and Arkhangelsk, with another 61 returned. In 158 sailings only one ship had been sunk (a second was torpedoed, but towed safely to port).

This was not to say the voyage was easy. The threat of enemy action was ever present, even if it had not posed a serious danger during 1941. German-occupied Norway and German-allied Finland offered nearby bases from which the *Kriegsmarine* (the German navy) and Luftwaffe could launch attacks, which therefore required a heavy escort for Russian convoys.

Nor was enemy action the only threat. Arctic conditions made the journey perilous at all times, with ice damage an ever-present threat that increased during the winter months, and Arctic storms another danger. A man going overboard in the Arctic Ocean or surrounding waters had only minutes to live before succumbing to hypothermia.

Yet the Arctic convoys were vital. Soviet Russia was Germany's biggest opponent, and if the Soviet Union surrendered Anglo-American chances of defeating Germany shrank dramatically. The Soviets had to be kept in the war. Much of the Soviet industrial belt was overrun by Germany, and while it was relocating war production east of the Urals, Russia faced critical shortages of weapons, ammunition, and all the hardware required for modern war.

The Western Allies had all the materiel in plenty, but the challenge lay in getting it to the Soviet Union. Three supply routes were available. One ran from the North American Pacific Coast to Vladivostok and from there to the battlefield through the Trans-Siberian Railroad. A second wound its way from Britain or North America around Africa into the Persian Gulf, across Iran and across the Caucuses or Caspian Sea. Both these routes were long and slow, and the Iranian route was just opening as 1942 began.

The shortest and fastest route ran by sea across the Arctic Ocean to Russian Arctic ports, but it was also the most perilous. Providing an adequate escort for Arctic convoys strained Allied naval resources requiring destroyers and antisubmarine craft to protect

Atlantic convoys from U-boats. Protection was also needed to prevent attacks by Focke-Wulf Condors. Arctic convoys passed within easy range of Kriegsmarine surface ships and Luftwaffe medium bombers, so cruisers and battleships were required as protection from the surface ships, and antiaircraft ships (including antiaircraft cruisers) were used to guard against air attack.

The most exposed part of the voyage was made without air cover. The nearest Coastal Command airfields to the Arctic run were in Iceland and the Shetlands, but land-based aircraft stationed there lacked the range to reach convoys north and east of Norway's Narvik harbour. The Soviet air forces might have provided air cover on the eastern end of the run, but the Soviets were reluctant to operate aircraft over open water and needed the limited aircraft they had to protect their own ports and cities. Aircraft carriers would have been welcome, but, in January 1942, the Royal Navy's fleet carriers were too valuable to risk on convoy escort duty. Furthermore, the Royal Navy had lost its only commissioned escort carrier in December 1941 and no more would be available until the last half of 1942.

Despite that, through to the end of February 1942, Arctic convoys successfully reached their destinations with minimal losses. But in March that began to change, owing to two British Commando raids the previous December. Hitler took the raids on Vågsoy Island and the Lofoten Islands, which took place on 26 and 27 December 1941, as precursors to a British invasion of Norway, and ordered warplanes, U-boats and warships to protect the country.

A major purpose of the raids was to draw German forces away from areas where the Allies intended to fight, but it succeeded too well. German ground forces sent to Norway were effectively removed from fighting theatres elsewhere, but German air and sea forces could now reach well beyond the Norwegian coastline, threatening the Allied convoys. Neither Admiral Erich Raeder of the Kriegsmarine nor Reichsmarschall Hermann Göring of the Luftwaffe wanted their forces in Scandinavia standing idle, and the Arctic convoys proved irresistible.

At first the Allied losses remained low. Despite the Royal Navy's concerns over what Kriegsmarine surface forces might do to convoys, that fear went largely unrealized over the first nine months of the Arctic run. Losses were mainly due to U-boats and the hazards of the sea, but then the Luftwaffe joined the fight. During March and April, the Luftwaffe's contribution was minor, but by May, and now carrying torpedoes as well as bombs, Luftwaffe bombers sank half the Allied ships lost during Convoy PQ-15. Having found their stride, the Luftwaffe became the true menace to Allied shipping, and their ability to find convoys grew with the lengthening Arctic summer days.

OPPOSITE STRATEGIC OVERVIEW

So did the peril faced by merchantmen on the Arctic run. Though the Allied naval commanders obsessed over the threat posed by the surface ships of the Kriegsmarine, at war's end the number of Allied ships sunk by these warships could be counted on the fingers of one hand. Meanwhile, however, U-boats and Luftwaffe bombers were ripping Arctic convoys apart. In July 1942, following an ill-advised dispersal of Convoy PQ-17 a massacre ensued in which 24 of the 38 merchant ships in the convoy were sunk. Three were lost before the convoy dispersed; 21 afterwards. Of that total, seven were sunk by Luftwaffe aircraft and nine crippled by bombers allowing them to be finished off by U-boats.

The Allies tried everything they could to counter the threat posed by the Luftwaffe. They added antiaircraft ships to the convoys, sent RAF units to Murmansk and the Kola Peninsula to attempt to close the Luftwaffe's bases through bombing, put Hurricane fighters on merchant ships equipped with catapults (this allowed a one-shot attack by the Hurricane, which had to ditch afterwards), and finally, they committed one of their scarce escort carriers to an Arctic convoy.

The climax came in September 1942, with convoy PQ-18. The Luftwaffe threw everything it could at the convoy, and the Allies retaliated in kind. A bloody fight ensued, at the end of which the convoy remained together but 30 per cent of the ships sent were sunk – over three-quarters of the losses were due to air attack.

The Luftwaffe lost 15 to 20 per cent of the aircraft it committed to the battle, but the Allies threw in the towel and suspended Arctic convoy sailing until December, relying on the long Arctic night to shield them from the Luftwaffe. They never again attempted an Arctic convoy during the summer months of June through August, due to the perceived threat of Luftwaffe aircraft. However, the Luftwaffe's tide ebbed as quickly as it rose. In November the Allies landed in North Africa in Operation *Torch*, and to counter this and a new British offensive in northeast Africa, the Luftwaffe's bombers harassing Arctic convoys were redeployed to the Mediterranean.

The Arctic convoys continued to face the twin perils of the Kriegsmarine's U-boats and surface warships but most of the aircraft remaining in the Arctic Circle were maritime reconnaissance. The Arctic run remained hazardous, but not nearly as hazardous as when the Luftwaffe was present in force. From December 1943 when convoys resumed until May 1945 when the war ended, aircraft sank only one ship sailing in an Arctic convoy, and sank only one more during an air raid on a Russian port.

The 1942 Arctic convoy battles proved to be the last successful air campaign of the Luftwaffe. Even there, success was tenuous. German success depended heavily on Allied reluctance to risk merchant convoys to the threat of German air attack – a threat that existed largely within the imagination of Allied planners. Regardless, the result constricted supplies sent by the Arctic route for the rest of the war.

This campaign was hard-fought by both sides, and the margin of victory narrow as both adversaries strove to meet their goals in one of the most inhospitable places in the globe. The Arctic was an area hostile to ships and even more unforgiving to aircraft – the environment as much a foe to each side as the enemy they were fighting. The men of both sides which fought this campaign were courageous and resolute, and all were tested to the limits of human endurance. This book tells their story.

Novaya Zemlya

Summer ice limits

Spitsbergen

Hope Island

Barents Sea

Bear Island

SOVIET UNION

Arkhangelsk

Iokanka

Murmansk

White Sea

FINLAND

Altenfjord

Narvik/Viestfjord

LOFTEN ISLANDS

SWEDEN

NORWAY

Trondheim

Greenland Sea

Greenland

Jan Mayen

Norwegian Sea

SHETLAND ISLANDS

FAROE ISLANDS

Summer ice limits

Winter ice limits

Denmark Strait

Seidisfjord

ICELAND

Reykjavik

● German bases
● Allied bases
--- Effective range of the Luftwaffe
─── Front line in 1942
░░░ Allied minefields

N

0   200 miles
0   200 km

CHRONOLOGY

1941

22 June Germany attacks the Soviet Union.

12 July Anglo-Soviet Agreement signed, obligating Britain to supply the Soviet Union with munitions.

21–31 August Convoy Dervish sails to Arkhangelsk, Russia, from Hvalfjörður, Iceland, beginning Arctic convoys to and from Russia.

28 September The PQ–QP convoy series opens with the sailing of Convoy QP-1 to Scapa Flow.

10 December United States declares war on Germany and Italy.

26–27 December Vågsoy Island and the Lofoten Islands raided by British commandos.

29 December Hitler decides the commando raids presage a British invasion of Norway, ordering Wehrmacht, Kriegsmarine and Luftwaffe reinforcements sent to the area.

1942

2 January The 5,135grt *Waziristan* becomes the first Arctic convoy ship lost.

17 January HMS *Matabele* sunk by *U-454*, the first British warship lost on the Arctic run.

24 January First *Kampfgeschwader* (KG) 30 aircraft arrive at Banak and Bardufoss.

March KG 26 begins transferring two Gruppes to Bardufoss and Banak.

December 1941 raids on Vågsoy Island (shown here) and the Lofoten Islands convinced Hitler the British planned an invasion of Norway. His orders led to reinforcement of Luftflotte 5 in Norway, making bombers available to attack Arctic convoys. (AC)

11 April Luftwaffe Ju 88s bomb Convoy QP-10, sinking 7,161grt cargo ship *Empire Cowper*. It is the first ship sunk in convoy by Luftwaffe aircraft.

14 April Luftwaffe dive bombers sink British steamship *Lancaster Castle* (5,172grt) in port after its arrival at Murmansk in PQ-12.

3 May Six He 111 bombers of KG 26 make the first Luftwaffe torpedo bomber attack of World War II. They hit three ships, sinking two and damaging a third.

21–30 May Convoy PQ-16 sails from Reykjavík to Murmansk. Constantly attacked by Luftwaffe aircraft, it loses six ships to aircraft with three damaged.

June Final Luftwaffe reinforcements arrive in Norway.

26 June Convoy QP-13 leaves Arkhangelsk. Despite being spotted by Luftwaffe reconnaissance, it is largely ignored due to the Germans concentrating on Convoy PQ-17.

27 June Convoy PQ-17 departs Reykjavík.

4 July Convoy PQ-17 ordered dispersed.

7 July Convoy QP-13 arrives at Reykjavík after losing five ships to a friendly minefield. These are the only casualties suffered by QP-13.

25 July Final five surviving ships from PQ-17 arrive in Arkhangelsk.

2 September Convoy PQ-18 departs Loch Ewe, Scotland for Murmansk.

13 September First Luftwaffe attack on PQ-18, including the war's first 'Goldene Zange' attack.

14–18 September Luftwaffe makes heavy attacks daily on Convoy PQ-18.

22 September PQ-19 is cancelled.

Two ships destined to play important roles in PQ-17 were the ASW trawler *Ayrshire* and the Hog Islander *Troubadour*. *Ayrshire* is shown in this photo taken from *Troubadour*'s deck. The M-3 tank in the foreground is part of *Troubadour*'s deck cargo. (USNHHC)

26 September PQ-18 arrives at Arkhangelsk, after losing ten of the convoy's 40 cargo ships to air attacks and two to U-boats.

29 October–3 November Operation *FB*, individual sailing by unescorted merchantmen, replaces escorted Arctic convoys.

8 November An Anglo-American army invades French North Africa as Operation *Torch* begins.

8–12 November Luftwaffe units begin transferring from Norway and Finland to the Mediterranean.

17 November PQ–QP series terminates with the sailing of QP-15 from Kola Inlet on 17 November and its arrival at Loch Ewe on 30 November.

15 December British resume Arctic convoys, with a new convoy code. Convoy JW-51A departs Liverpool for Murmansk.

31 December Battle of Barents Sea fought. Two British light cruisers drive *Lützow* and *Admiral Hipper* away from Convoy JW-51B.

1943
2 March 12 KG 30 Ju 88s attack RA-53, the first Luftwaffe attack on an Arctic convoy at sea since PQ-18, but sink no ships.

26 December Battle of North Cape, *Scharnhorst* sunk attempting to attack JW-55B.

1944
September KG 26 begins transferring back to Norway.

1945
7 February KG 26 sends a 48 aircraft strike against JW-63, its first since returning to Norway. It fails to find the convoy.

10 February 32 KG 26 torpedo bombers attack JW-63. They score no hits, and lose five aircraft.

23 February Liberty Ship *Henry Bacon* becomes the last ship sunk in an Arctic convoy by Luftwaffe aircraft, and the first to be sunk at sea since the resumption of convoys in December 1943. It is the last ship lost on the Arctic run.

7 May Germany surrenders to the United Nations.

30 May Final Arctic convoy, RA-53, arrives at Clyde.

The real danger on the Arctic run came from the foe the Allies were least able to fight in 1942: Luftwaffe aircraft. A lack of air cover and inadequate antiaircraft defences enabled the Luftwaffe to attack convoys with relative impunity during this year. (AC)

ATTACKER'S CAPABILITIES
The Luftwaffe's maritime strike force

Aircraft

The Luftwaffe was initially conceived as a bomber force to support Wehrmacht operations; maritime patrol and strike was largely added after World War II began but, by the beginning of 1942, the Luftwaffe had gained proficiency in both.

The most significant aircraft used in this campaign were the Luftwaffe's main medium bombers, the Heinkel 111 and the Ju 88. These aircraft were used most frequently to attack Allied convoys. They were supplemented by pre-war Luftwaffe maritime patrol aircraft, such as the Heinkel He 115 and the Blohm & Voss BV 138, as well as the wartime-developed Focke-Wulf 200. These were used primarily for reconnaissance, although the He 115 did occasionally attack convoys, especially after being adapted to a torpedo-bomber role.

Luftwaffe single- and multi-engine fighters played minor roles in this campaign, as did single-engine strike and reconnaissance aircraft. Limited Allied aircraft presence with Arctic convoys during 1942 gave fighters like the Messerschmitt Bf 109 and Bf 110, or the Focke-Wulf 190, little scope for action. These aircraft protected German bases in Scandinavia from Allied bombers or escorted bombing raids against northern Russian ports. Similarly, the limited range of the Arado Ar 196 meant its reconnaissance role was better served by multi-engine patrol aircraft. Only the Junkers Ju 87 saw use, and that largely against ships in Russian ports or close to the Scandinavian coast.

The aircraft most involved in interdicting the Allies' Arctic convoys to Russia were:

Junkers Ju 88: The Ju 88 was the Luftwaffe's most versatile aircraft, serving as a bomber, dive bomber, torpedo bomber, reconnaissance aircraft, night fighter and heavy fighter during World War II. With twin-engines, it had a crew of four as a bomber. Its length was 14.36m (47.1ft), its wingspan 20.08m (65.9ft). It had a 470km/h (290mph) top speed, a 370km/h (230mph) cruising speed, a 1,790km (1,110 miles) operational range and a service ceiling of 8,200m (26,900ft). As a bomber it could carry up to 1,400kg (3,100lb) of bombs internally and up to 3,000kg (6,600lb) externally. It could be modified to carry

The Ju 88 was Nazi Germany's most versatile aircraft, deployed in almost every role except transport. It was an important tool in the Luftwaffe's campaign against Arctic convoys, serving as a bomber, torpedo bomber and reconnaissance aircraft. (AC)

two torpedoes. It had five MG 81 7.92mm machine guns, three in flexible single mounts firing from the nose and ventral positions fore and aft, and a dorsal flexible twin mount at the aft cockpit.

The Germans called the Ju 88 *Mädchen für Alles* (Maid of all Work) due to its flexibility. It had been strengthened and modified pre-war to serve as a heavy dive bomber. Other models were also modified to serve as reconnaissance aircraft, radar-equipped night fighters (with upward-firing *Schrage-Musik* 20mm cannon) and as heavy fighters with up to six 20mm forward-firing cannon in the nose. Against Arctic convoys, the Ju 88 was primarily used for reconnaissance, and as a bomber, both a dive bomber and torpedo bomber.

Heinkel He 111: The He 111 twin-engine bomber was Germany's main medium bomber through most of World War II. Its length was 16.4m (53.8ft) with a 22.6m (74.15ft) wingspan. It had a 440km/h (270mph) top speed, a cruising speed with a full bomb load of 300km/h (190mph), a 2,300km (1,400 miles) range and a 6,500m (21,300ft) service ceiling. It could carry up to 2,000kg (4,400lb) of bombs internally, or 3,600kg (7,900lb) or two torpedoes on external racks. (It could not carry bombs internally with external racks attached.) For defensive armament it carried six or seven MG 15 or MG 81 7.92mm (.30cal) machine guns and one MG 151 13mm machine gun in single-mount hand-held positions.

It first flew in 1935, disguised as a civilian airliner, though military versions appeared in 1936. Although it was upgraded throughout production, by 1942 it was obsolete, but despite this, production continued until 1944. Equipped with torpedoes or bombs, it served satisfactorily against convoys without air cover. It was primarily used as a torpedo bomber against Arctic convoys.

Heinkel He 115: The twin-engine He 115 was a floatplane maritime patrol aircraft. It was frequently used for reconnaissance, but also used as a torpedo bomber and a minelaying aircraft. It had a crew of three, was 17.3m (56.75ft) long with a wingspan of 22.28m (73.08ft). It had a combat range of 2,100km (1,300 miles), a service ceiling of 5,200m (17,100ft), a maximum speed of 327km/h (203mph), a cruising speed of 280km/h (174mph) and a maximum endurance of 18 hours. It could carry up to 1,250kg (2,750lb) of bombs, one torpedo or one 920kg (2,000lb) sea mine. It was armed with one flexible MG 17 and one MG 15 7.93mm machine guns, in nose and dorsal mounts.

The He 115 was ordered in 1935, and first flew in 1937, entering operational service in 1939. By 1941, 138 had been built, with production restarting in 1943. Considered the best floatplane of World War II, the He 115 was a torpedo bomber and reconnaissance aircraft in the Arctic.

Blohm & Voss BV 138: The Blohm & Voss BV 138 *Seedrache* (Sea Dragon) was a tri-motor flying boat used for long-range maritime patrol. It was 19.85m (65.08ft) long, with a 26.94m (88.4ft) wingspan. It had a 285km/h (177mph) top speed, a 235 km/h (146mph) cruising speed, an operational range of 1,220km (760 miles) at 195km/h (121mph), a relatively short six-hour endurance and a 5,000m (16,400ft) service ceiling. It had a six-man crew and carried a defensive armament of two 20mm MG 151 cannon individually mounted in power nose and tail turrets, and a single 13mm MG 131 machine gun in an open ring mount behind the centre engine. Primarily a reconnaissance aircraft, it could carry up to six 50kg (110lb) bombs under the wings.

First flown in 1937, it became operational in 1940, and 297 were built between 1938 and 1943. It had an odd appearance with a short fuselage, two engines mounted mid-wing in nacelles forming twin booms holding the horizontal and vertical stabilizers, and the centre engine mounted above the fuselage in a streamlined fairing. Its side profile gave it the appearance of a shoe, giving rise to the nickname *Der Fliegende Holzschuh* (Flying clog) a play on the name *Der Fliegende Hollander* (The Flying Dutchman).

Focke-Wulf Fw 200: The Fw 200 Condor was a very-long-range maritime patrol aircraft. It had a 360km/h (223mph) top speed, a 335km/h (208mph) cruising speed, a service ceiling of 6,000m (20,000ft), a 3,560km (2,210 mile) range and a 14 hour endurance. Its wingspan was 32.85m (107.77ft) and its length 23.45m (77ft). It was armed with an MG 151 20mm cannon in the forward ventral gondola, an MG 131 13mm machine gun in a hand-held aft dorsal mount and four MG 15 7.9mm machine guns individually mounted in a power top turret, and flexible beam and aft ventral mountings. It had a maximum bomb load of 5,400kg (4,620lb) on wing mounts or 1,000kg (2,200lb) internally, but generally carried less for greater range. It had a crew of five to seven.

Originally an airliner, it was converted to military use by attaching a bomb bay beneath the fuselage and adding machine guns and cannon for anti-shipping and air-to-air defence. The Condor was structurally weak and virtually helpless against fighters (or even Allied patrol bombers), but became the terror of the Atlantic in 1940 by operating against largely unarmed merchantmen sailing individually. By 1942 its reign as an attack aircraft was over, though it remained a superb maritime patrol aircraft due to its endurance and long range, and was so used on Arctic convoys.

Junkers Ju 87: A two place, single-engine dive bomber, the Junkers Ju 87 Stuka (short for *Sturzkampfflugzeug* 'dive bomber') was a dive bomber developed as an army ground support aircraft, though it proved effective against maritime targets during the war's opening months. It had a 383km/h (238mph) top speed, a 209km/h (130mph) cruising speed, an 8,200m (26,900ft) operational ceiling and a 595.5km (370 mile) range when carrying bombs. It was armed with two fixed forward-firing MG 17 7.92mm and one flexible rear-mounted MG 15 7.29mm machine gun. It carried a centre-mounted 250kg (550lb) bomb and four wing-mounted 50 kg (110lb) bombs.

The Ju 87 was World War II's iconic Luftwaffe aircraft. A low-wing metal monoplane, with inverted gull-wings and fixed landing gear in faired housings, it looked like a predatory hawk. An accurate dive bomber, it was deadly against unarmed opponents, but it was also slow, had limited manoeuvrability and weak defensive armament, making it vulnerable to fighters. Its short range limited its usefulness in maritime roles, but it did attack Arctic convoys close to German-held shores.

The He 111 was the Luftwaffe's main medium bomber when World War II began. One Gruppe, KG 26, converted to carrying aerial torpedoes. These aircraft saw extensive service in the Arctic, proving a hazard to Allied shipping. (AC)

OPPOSITE GERMAN AND ALLIED AIRFIELDS

Facilities and infrastructure

The Germans faced two obstacles in conducting an aerial offensive against Arctic convoys: possessing adequate facilities from which to mount the offensive and then developing the infrastructure to support and supply those facilities.

The path to Russia through the Arctic crossed one of the world's most hostile environments – even during summer months it was cold and inhospitable. The lands bordering Arctic waters were a frozen desert most of the year, and plains upon which airfields could be built frequently became bogs during the brief Arctic summer.

The population of Finnmark, then Norway's northernmost county, was sparse at the beginning of World War II. There were few communities, and those that did exist had populations numbering only in the hundreds – for example, the population of Vadsø, the region's administrative centre, was under 2,000 in 1940. Little existing infrastructure could support airfields and naval ports, and conditions in Northern Finland were little better. Northern Lapland was just as sparsely populated as Finnmark, with its largest town, the port city of Petsamo, about as large as Vadsø.

As 1942 began, the Luftwaffe had a series of airfields and seaplane bases throughout Norway and Finland – a combination of bases which existed prior to the 1940 Winter War between Finland and the Soviet Union and the 1940 occupation of Norway, and those built for the Luftwaffe after occupation. Additionally, Sola Airfield at Stavanger and Værnes Airfield in Trondheim supported Luftwaffe activities against Arctic convoys by providing bases for long-range maritime reconnaissance aircraft.

The most important northern airfields included Kirkenes, Banak, Bardufoss and Bodö in Finnmark, and Petsamo in Lapland. Banak, Bodö and Bardufoss were existing Norwegian airfields taken over by Germany after conquest, and similarly, Petsamo was one of six pre-war airfields in Lapland. The major seaplane stations and anchorages which were used in this campaign included Alta-See and Tromsø, though there were also seaplane facilities associated with Bodö, Kirkenes, Stavanger and Trondheim.

None of these airfields, except Stavanger, were well developed prior to World War II. Stavanger had a concrete runway, but the rest were unpaved, with Banak, Bardufoss and Bodö having been built in the late 1930s by the Norwegians to protect Finnmark from a potential Soviet invasion. They had either gravel or turf runways in 1940, as did the airfields

Luftwaffe aircraft operated under primitive conditions out of Finnmark airfields. The airfields had gravel or wood-plank runways and maintenance facilities were crude. Fuelling and servicing had to be done outdoors in a harsh climate. (AC)

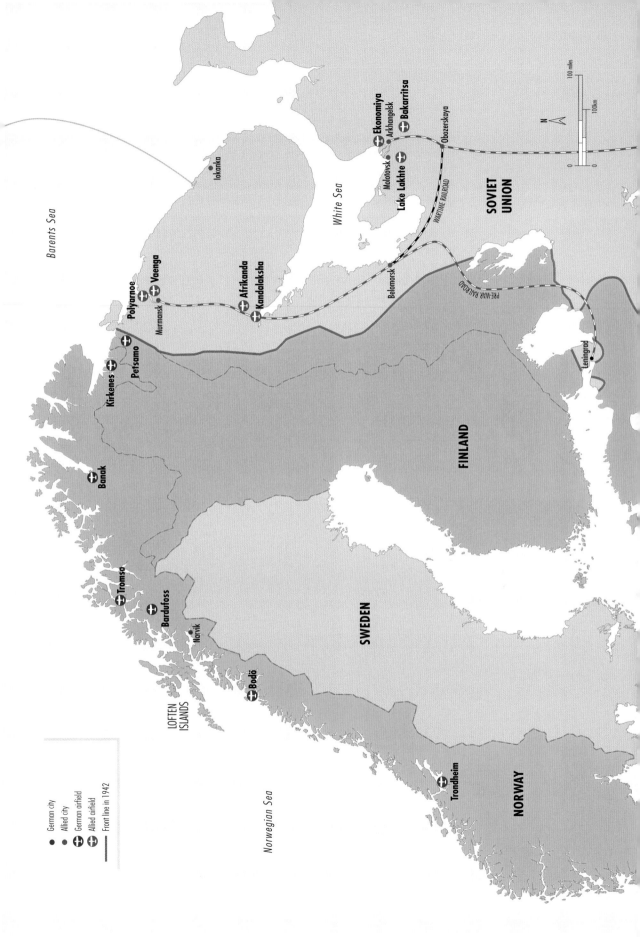

Barents Sea

Iokanka

White Sea

Ekonomiya ✠
Arkhangelsk ●
Bakaritsa ✠
Molotovsk ●
Obozerskaya ✠
Lake Lakhte ✠

WARTIME RAILROAD

SOVIET
UNION

100 miles
100km

N

Polyarnoe ✠
Vaenga ✠
Murmansk ●
Afrikanda ✠
Kandalaksha ✠

Belomorsk ●

PRE-WAR RAILROAD

Kirkenes ✠
Petsamo ✠

Leningrad ●

Banak ✠

FINLAND

Tromsø ✠
Bardufoss ✠
Narvik ●

SWEDEN

Bodö ✠

LOFTEN
ISLANDS

Norwegian Sea

Trondheim ✠

NORWAY

● German city
● Allied city
✠ ✠ German airfield
✠ ✠ Allied airfield
▬ Front line in 1942

around Trondheim. Petsamo, along with the other five Lapland airfields, were little more than cleared fields with a few small buildings or sheds for support.

Between the start of the German occupation and the invasion of Russia in June 1941, the Germans extensively improved their airfields in Norway. At first, airfields in southern and central Norway, including Trondheim, were improved to support the Battle of Britain; however, as the Germans prepared to invade Russia, they also upgraded airfields in Finnmark. The Luftwaffe improved Finnish airfields after Finland declared war on the Soviet Union in June 1941, and by January 1942 these were able to support a broad range of Luftwaffe aircraft, even multi-engine aircraft.

However, even these improvements were more rudimentary than seen elsewhere in Europe. Banak's two main runways had wooden-plank surfacing, as did Petsamo, and Kirkenes had only dirt and gravel-surfaced runways throughout its existence. Trondheim, Bardufoss and Bodö gained concrete runways between 1940 and the middle of 1942, although Bodö's runways were partly wood and partly concrete, while its taxiways were wooden. All had buildings permitting maintenance and rudimentary repair of aircraft, as well as fuelling and ammunition storage facilities, and aircraft dispersal areas.

Tromsø, a pre-war Norwegian Naval Air Service Station, was the Luftwaffe's main seaplane station in northern Norway. It had 30 mooring buoys, jetties for fuel and ammunition, and a large double hangar with attached workshop and concrete apron. Alta-See was primarily a seaplane anchorage with basic fuel and ammunition capabilities, but no maintenance facilities, and Bodö-See was a refuelling stop. In 1942, Kirkenes's seaplane facilities were just an anchorage, whereas Trondheim and Stavanger had extensive seaplane facilities used mainly by long-range reconnaissance seaplanes involved with Arctic convoys.

The Luftwaffe's infrastructure supporting their forces in Finnmark and Lapland were as ad hoc and improvised as their airfields and facilities. One problem faced by forces in the far north, Axis and Allies alike, was that it was at the end of a long supply line. Everything

Tromsø was the Luftwaffe's main seaplane station in northern Norway. It had pre-war mooring buoys and maintenance jetties, but Arctic conditions made it difficult to operate from. A BV 138 is being towed ashore, and an He 115 can be seen in the background. (USNHHC)

except drinking water, including rations, arms and materiel, had to be shipped there by sea. No railroads ran to Finnmark or Lapland, and roads were poor in summer and impassable in winter.

Although Norway's west and north coast remained ice-free during the winter, logistics were complicated by the relatively small merchant marine available to the Axis in Scandinavia. Furthermore, the Luftwaffe was not the only organization requiring use of Germany's sealift capabilities – multiple demands fell on it. The Wehrmacht was pursuing a land offensive to capture Murmansk and the Kola Peninsula in 1941 and 1942, and so the Kriegsmarine maintained a large naval presence in Norway. It kept its major surface units in Trondheim and the northern ports in 1942 and 1943, and the 13th U-boat Flotilla operated out of Trondheim during this period. Furthermore, Narvik was an ice-free port from which Swedish iron ore went to Germany and was an anchorage (along with Alten Fjord) for Kriegsmarine warships attacking the Arctic convoys.

Additionally, the German merchant marine did not grow to meet demands for greater shipping, but instead shrank as the hazards of the sea took a toll. Furthermore, to protect Allied Arctic convoys, the Royal Navy maintained heavy submarine patrols off Norwegian coastal waters whose main targets were major Kriegsmarine warships (especially the battleship *Tirpitz*), but few submarine commanders ignored merchant targets when encountered.

The Luftwaffe could only maintain a maximum of 300–400 aircraft in the Arctic. That limit was mitigated by two factors: the ability to stage aircraft from southern Scandinavia and the number of aircraft available to the Luftwaffe.

Staging involved operating aircraft out of airfields in southern or central Norway to support actions in the Arctic. Aircraft would be maintained, serviced and armed in airfields such as Stavanger's Sola or Trondheim, and flown to airfields in Finnmark where they refuelled to attack the convoy. Returning to the Finnmark airfields they might be rearmed and refuelled

Narvik was northern Norway's most important harbour, serving as the point from which Swedish iron ore was shipped to Germany. It served as a Kriegsmarine anchorage, although it lacked repair facilities to make it a full naval port. (AC)

OPPOSITE *DIE GOLDENE ZANGE* (THE GOLDEN COMB)

The Golden Comb used a line of torpedo bombers flying line abreast at 50m intervals, and simultaneously releasing torpedoes. With 46 bombers, this sent 92 torpedoes in a line over a nautical mile long racing towards a convoy. This 3D view shows what the Germans hoped would happen – that the convoy moved forwards without evading the torpedoes. In reality, the convoy commodore ordered a hard left turn. Only the right two columns failed to turn and six of the eight ships hit were in those columns.

for another attack or flown back to southern bases for servicing, depending upon whether this was needed.

The period during which a convoy could be attacked by aircraft was brief – rarely more than a week. Staging minimized the time aircraft spent in the far north, reducing the logistical demands at the Finnmark air bases. Additionally, very-long-range patrol aircraft, such as the He 115 or Fw 200 could operate effectively out of Stavanger, Bergen or Trondheim.

The real reason logistical limitation never constrained Luftwaffe Arctic operations was that the Luftwaffe lacked the aircraft to commit enough to strain logistic limits. By January 1942 the Luftwaffe had to maintain a presence supporting air activities in Russia, the Mediterranean, France and Germany, and 200–250 multi-engine aircraft were as much as could be committed in Norway and Lapland. Even in Lapland, most of the Luftwaffe's effort went towards supporting German ground offensives. Germany could get enough ammunition, fuel and supplies to support their aircraft simply because they had relatively few aircraft to support.

Weapons and tactics

Luftwaffe bombers used bombs and torpedoes offensively to attack and sink ships in Allied Arctic convoys, but they also deployed a variety of cannon and machine guns to defend their aircraft and, less often, to strafe shipping. While the Luftwaffe had a wide variety of specialist bombs, those most frequently used against Allied merchant ships and warships were 50kg and 250kg high explosive bombs.

The most common bomb used was one that all Luftwaffe bombers could carry, the SC 250 (*Sprengbombe Cylindrisch 250* – the number indicated its weight in kilograms). Total weight was 250kg (550lb), 130kg (290lb) of which was the explosive filling (typically TNT, Amatol or Trialen – Trialen was the explosive most often employed against shipping). The outer shell was made of cast, tube or forged steel. Grade I bombs, intended to penetrate, had the nose and main body forged from a single piece of steel, whereas Grade II and III bombs consisted of three steel sections – nose cone, body and aft cone – welded together. All had a four-finned tail attached after the bomb was filled. A single SC 250, properly placed, could sink a typical merchantman.

The SC 50 was also used against shipping, although they would more likely be used against stragglers or crippled vessels, sailing independently. It held 16.4kg (36lb) of explosive, and was generally filled with TNT, Amatol or Trialen. Anti-ship SC 50s were fitted with anti-ricochet adapters to prevent them from bouncing off targets. It typically took multiple hits from SC 50s to sink all but the smallest seagoing vessels.

In 1942 the Luftwaffe's primary aerial torpedo was the 45cm diameter F5b torpedo. It carried a 180–250kg (397–551lb) Hexanite warhead, capable of sinking an Allied merchantman with one hit. It could travel 2,000m (6,500ft) at a 40-knot setting or 6,000m (19,500ft) at 24 knots. It used hydrogen peroxide as the oxidant and Decalin (decahydronaphthalene) fuel. Total weight was 725–812kg (1,598–1,790lb), and its overall length was 4.804–5.160m (15.75ft–16.96ft) – the warhead fitted accounted for differences in length and weight. This torpedo had a wooden tail attached to stabilize flight while in the air which broke off once the torpedo entered the water. The torpedo

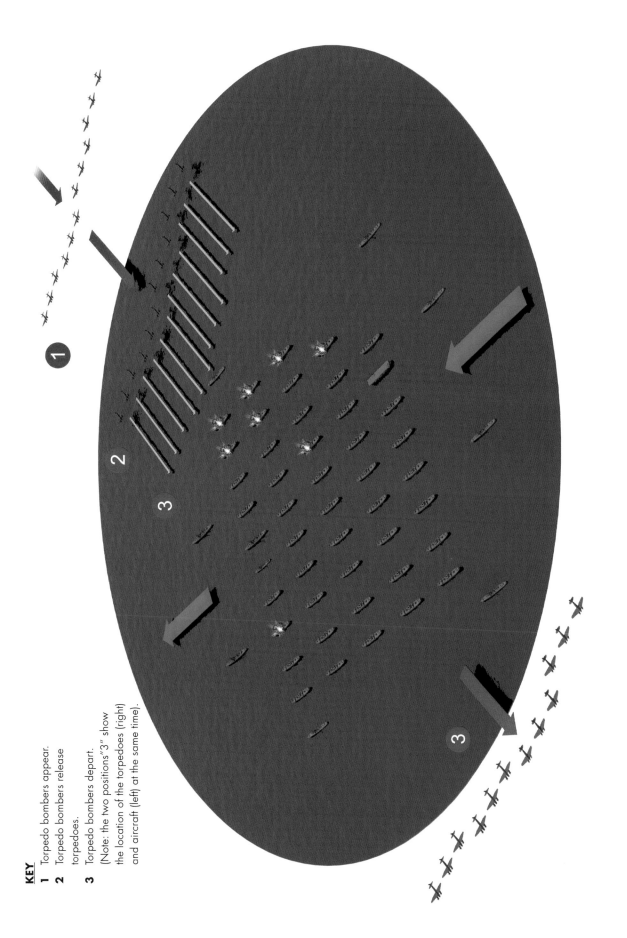

KEY
1 Torpedo bombers appear.
2 Torpedo bombers release torpedoes.
3 Torpedo bombers depart.
(Note: the two positions "3" show the location of the torpedoes (right) and aircraft (left) at the same time).

had to be dropped at speeds less than 250km/h (155mph) and from no higher than 40m (131ft).

Luftwaffe aircraft involved in this campaign were armed with MG 15, MG 17, MG 81 and MG 131 machine guns, and MG 151/20 cannon. The MG 15, MG 17 and MG 81 were all 7.92mm machine guns firing rifle calibre bullets. The MG 131 was a 13mm machine gun, and the MG 151 a 20mm autocannon.

The MG 15 and MG 17 were the same basic gun developed from the MG 30, an air-cooled, recoil-operated weapon firing a standard 7.92x57mm Mauser cartridge which fired an 11.7–12.7g bullet. The MG 15 was designed for a hand-held flexible mount while the MG 17 was used in fixed mountings. The MG 15 had a shorter barrel, lower muzzle velocity and rate of fire 20 per cent lower than the MG 17. The MG 15 had a 75-round drum, while the MG 17 used a 1,000-round belt.

The MG 81 was the aviation version of the MG 34, an upgraded MG 30. It was also a 7.92mm gun firing the standard 7.92x57mm Mauser cartridge. It had a higher rate of fire than the MG 17, was belt-fed and replaced the MG 15 for flexible mountings.

The MG 131 was developed by Rheinmetall in 1938, entering service in 1940. It was a lightweight 13mm gun, weighing 16.6kg (37lb), and could be used fixed or on flexible mountings. It fired a 38.5g round, air-cooled and recoil-operated. The round was not just heavier than that of the 7.92mm, but it also fired an HEI (high-explosive, incendiary) round, similar to that fired by 20mm cannon.

The MG 151/20 was an upgrade of the original 15mm MG 151 autocannon designed for use on Luftwaffe fighters pre-war. Combat experience showed a larger explosive shell performed better, despite a lower muzzle velocity than the 15mm version. The MG 151/20 entered production in 1941. Although intended as a fixed weapon on fighters, it was used on flexible mountings on the Fw 200 and BV 138. It fired armour-piercing and high-explosive rounds, which weighed between 94g and 117g (3.3–4.1oz).

By 1942 the Luftwaffe had developed anti-shipping tactics through experience gained in the North Sea, Mediterranean Sea, Atlantic Ocean and English Channel. The preferred weapon against warships and merchant vessels were bombs, and while level bombing was used, dive bombing proved more effective and was preferred, especially against well-defended targets, like warships. The Luftwaffe introduced aerial torpedoes in 1942, and were still developing torpedo doctrine at that time.

With Arctic convoys, the preferred targets were merchant ships, and higher priority was given to inbound ships laden with munitions and supplies for the Soviets. The Luftwaffe however did not avoid warships or ignore outbound QP convoys – they attacked and sank these many times in 1942. The favoured target, laden or in ballast, was a solitary merchantman, a cripple or a straggler. In 1942 individual merchantmen rarely had significant antiaircraft guns, allowing an attacking aircraft to make multiple attacks, dropping bombs individually. Aircraft armed with 13mm machine guns or 20mm autocannon could strafe to good effect, and both guns could penetrate a merchantman's hull plating, possibly even sinking a ship.

Ships in convoy were more difficult targets, especially after the British began adding antiaircraft warships as escorts. Furthermore, the Arctic was even more inhospitable to aircraft than ships, and any damage incurred by an aircraft which prevented it returning safely to base was almost always fatal to their crews – aircraft lacked lifeboats and individual survival in Arctic waters was measured in

The SC 250 (Sprengbombe Cylindrisch 250) was the bomb most-commonly used by the Luftwaffe during their Arctic campaign. It weighed 250kg (550lb) of which 130kg (290lb) was explosive. (NMAF)

minutes. It soon became clear that saturating convoy defences with mass attacks minimized aircraft losses.

Conventional bombs could be delivered via level bombing, glide bombing or dive bombing. Level bombing required flying straight at a constant altitude to aim bombs, and worked well against stationary targets, but ships could manoeuvre to avoid the bombs. The higher the altitude the bombs were dropped, the longer it took for them to reach sea level – bombs dropped from altitudes above 5,000ft typically missed the intended target ship as it had time to manoeuvre away. However, in the crowded waters of a convoy it might hit another ship, and the manoeuvring served to disrupt the convoy.

Glide bombing and dive bombing had attacking bombers dive to hit the target. Glide bombing was typically conducted at a 20–40 degree dive, whereas dive bombing involved a dive greater than 45 degrees. In either attack the bomb followed the trajectory of the dive; the greater the dive angle the more likely an accurately aimed bomb was to hit, and gravitational effects on the trajectory shrank as the dive angle approached perpendicular. In reality, few dive bomb attacks were made at greater than a 75-degree angle, although the Stuka could dive vertically. The steeper the dive, the more difficult it became for antiaircraft to hit the attacking dive bomber.

The Luftwaffe added torpedoes to its aerial arsenal late, not introducing an air-dropped torpedo to operational status until December 1941. Training and conversion issues meant it was not fully deployed in the Arctic until June 1942. (AC)

However, dive bombing stressed the aircraft at pullout. Only two Luftwaffe aircraft were capable of acting as true dive bombers: the Ju 87 Stuka and the Ju 88. Others, including the He 111 and He 115, and the BV-138, were capable only of glide bombing, in which, like low-level horizontal bombing, aircraft were left vulnerable to antiaircraft fire, especially light antiaircraft fire.

Torpedo bombing duplicated several disadvantages of glide and horizontal bombing. Torpedo bombers had to fly a straight line at a low altitude and slowly enough to drop the torpedo without destroying it. That made them easier to shoot down since warships could fire their main guns at the torpedo bombers. Also, flying a torpedo bomber into a water column kicked up by a 5in, 6in or 8in shell striking the water would bring down the aircraft.

The advantages of torpedo attacks outweighed those drawbacks however. A single torpedo hit would almost certainly sink a cargo ship and cripple a warship, immobilizing it. Furthermore, a torpedo did not need to hit the ship it was aimed at – if it missed a ship in the convoy column closest to the bomber, it passed through each successive column, potentially finding a hit. The best defence against torpedoes was to turn parallel to its direction of travel, but in a crowded convoy this risked collision or incurring disorder. As a result, torpedo bombers often split, attacking from different directions and making it impossible to turn perpendicular to both sets of torpedoes.

By August the Luftwaffe had developed a mass-torpedo attack tactic called *die Goldene Zange* (the Golden Comb). Attacks were ideally made at dawn or dusk twilight, and the attacking torpedo bombers formed line abreast with aircraft 30m (100ft) apart. The line approached the convoy from abeam, aiming at its forward quarter, and all aircraft would drop torpedoes simultaneously, leaving a narrowly spaced line streaking towards the convoy. As many as 80 torpedoes were dropped in Golden Comb attacks, leaving a row of trails similar in appearance to the teeth of a comb.

DEFENDER'S CAPABILITIES

Fighting power of the convoy

Aircraft

The Hawker Hurricane was the most important British fighter used in this campaign. Used aboard CAM ships as the Hurricat and on escort carriers, it was also the fighter most frequently shipped to Russia. These RAF Hurricanes were operating out of Russia in 1941. (Wikimedia Commons)

Aircraft involved in defending the Arctic convoys were almost all British, belonging to the Royal Air Force or the Royal Navy's Fleet Air Arm. The Soviet Air Force or *Voyenno-Vozdushnye Sily* (VVS) played little role in the campaign since, in 1942, they had limited resources, with much of their pre-war air force destroyed during 1941. The surviving pilots were largely inexperienced and untrained in maritime patrol, and the Soviet command was reluctant to use resources to protect Allied ships. Additionally, the primary Arctic port (and the only one available during winter months), Murmansk, was only 32 miles from the nearest German airfields. This provided too little time for the Soviet Air Force to effectively launch fighters to protect ships in harbour.

British aircraft were limited by geography and infrastructure. Only ship-borne aircraft and land-based aircraft permitted to operate from Russian airfields could participate in the protection of Arctic convoys. Yet the British aircraft present had an influence on the battle out of proportion to their small numbers. Five aircraft types saw service in the Arctic in this campaign: the Hawker Sea Hurricane, the Fairey Swordfish and Albacore, the Consolidated Catalina and the Handley Page Hampden.

Hawker Sea Hurricane: The Sea Hurricane was a single-engine, single-seat fighter; a naval version of the land-based Hurricane with similar performance. Its length was 9.83m (32.25ft), its wingspan 12.19m (40ft). It had a 550km/h (340mph) top speed, a 375km/h (238mph) cruising speed, a 970km (600 mile) operational range and a service ceiling of 11,000m (36,000ft). Naval versions were armed with eight .303in (7.7mm) Browning machine guns.

The Hurricane was one of Britain's two standard RAF fighters when World War II began. While inferior to the Spitfire, it could hold its own against German fighters and was also simpler to maintain and more rugged than the other fighter. Due to a shortage of suitable British naval fighters, Hurricanes were converted for naval service, and there were two versions used in this campaign: the Sea Hurricane Mk IA and Sea Hurricane Mk IB. Both were conversions from the land-based Hurricane Mk I.

The Mk IA was intended for use on Catapult Armed Merchantmen (CAM) ships. They were modified to permit them to be catapulted off a ship when enemy aircraft were at hand and the pilot typically bailed out or ditched when the mission ended. Informally known as Hurricats, they were typically converted from older aircraft at the end of their service life. A total of 250 were converted.

The Mk IB was similarly modified for sea service. Equipped with an arrester hook they could operate off aircraft carriers and first entered service in July 1941. They saw service during the Arctic campaign aboard escort carrier *Avenger* during PQ-18. In total 340 Hurricanes were converted to Sea Hurricanes Mk IB.

Fairey Albacore: The Albacore was a single-engine biplane torpedo bomber, with fixed landing gear, and a crew of two. It was 12.22m (40.09ft) long with a 15.24m (50ft) wingspan, a 259km/h (161mph) top speed, a 230km/h (140mph) cruising speed, a service ceiling of 5,700m (18,800ft) and an effective range of 1,497km (930 miles) with torpedo. It was armed with one fixed, forward-firing .303cal M1919 Browning machine gun and one or two flexible .303cal Vickers machine guns in the rear cockpit. It could carry one 760kg (1,670lb) torpedo or up to 900kg (2,000lb) of bombs. It was to replace the Swordfish as the Royal Navy's torpedo bomber, but the closed-cockpit Albacore was in fact retired first. In the Arctic it was used briefly by fleet carriers in the covering forces to attack Kriegsmarine warships.

Fairey Swordfish: The Swordfish was the second-most important aircraft in guarding Arctic convoys. A single-engine biplane with fixed landing gear, a crew of two or three, it was originally designed as a torpedo bomber. It was 10.87m (35.67ft) long with a 13.87m (45.5ft) wingspan. Its maximum speed armed was 230km/h (143mph), with a 210km/h (131mph) cruising speed, with a service ceiling of 5,000m (16,500ft), an effective range of 840km (522 miles) and an endurance of 5 hours 30 minutes. It was armed with one fixed, forward-firing .303cal Vickers machine gun and a flexible .303cal Lewis or Vickers machine gun in the rear cockpit. It could carry one 760kg (1,670lb) torpedo or up to 700kg (1,500lb) of bombs, mines or depth charges. Starting in 1943 it was also armed with eight 60lb rockets in underwing mountings.

The open-cockpit Swordfish ended up serving in just about every role except fighter in its Fleet Air Arm career, including reconnaissance, artillery spotting, antisubmarine warfare (ASW) and even dive bombing. During Arctic convoys, radar-equipped Swordfish served as ASW aircraft.

The Handley Page Hampden began World War II as one of the RAF's three 'heavy' bombers. Relegated to second-rate status it was repurposed as a torpedo bomber. Hampdens were sent to Russia in August 1942, not to fight the Luftwaffe but to attack the Kriegsmarine. (AC)

Handley Page Hampden: The Hampden was a twin-engine RAF medium bomber. It had a crew of four with a 16.33m (53.6ft) length and a 21.08m (69.17ft) wingspan. It had a 398km/h (247mph) top speed, a 332km/h (206mph) cruising speed and a 2,770km (1,720 mile) range. For defence it carried one fixed, forward-firing .303cal M1919 Browning machine gun and three flexible .303cal Vickers machine guns in the nose and one or two each in dorsal and ventral positions. It could carry one 760kg (1,670lb) torpedo or up to 1,800kg (4,000lb) of bombs.

One of three main RAF medium bombers in 1939, it was obsolescent as a bomber when 1942 began. In April 1942 two squadrons were transferred to Coastal Command for use as torpedo bombers and were moved to Russia in the summer of that year, where they operated out of Soviet airfields, hunting Kriegsmarine battleships, battlecruisers and cruisers. After PQ-18 and the suspension of Arctic convoys until winter, the aircraft were turned over to the Soviets and the crews withdrawn to Britain.

Consolidated Catalina: The Catalina was a twin-engine, parasol-wing flying boat with a crew of ten. Later versions were amphibious, capable of landing on either land or water. It was 19.48m (63.9ft) long with a 32m (104ft) wingspan. Slow, with a 315km/h (196mph) top speed and a 201km/h (125mph) cruising speed, it had an extremely long range, 4,060km (2,520 miles), and a 4,800m (15,800ft) service ceiling. Extremely reliable, it could carry 1,800kg (4,000lb) of bombs, depth charges or torpedoes. British versions were armed with seven .303 machine guns, and it could be equipped with radar.

The Catalina entered British service in March 1941. Coastal Command 201 Squadron operated Catalinas out of Grasnaya, a Soviet base in the Kola inlet. Catalinas were extremely effective antisubmarine and maritime reconnaissance aircraft, and were used for both during their 1942 service in the Arctic, although their primary focus was scouting Kriegsmarine surface warships. The Catalina was a United States import.

Facilities and infrastructure

If the Germans had difficulties with their facilities and infrastructure in the Arctic campaign, the Allied forces involved in convoying supplies to Russia via the Arctic route also had problems obtaining their own facilities and infrastructure within the area. In fact, the Allies had no bases in the area, and the Soviets were almost as suspicious of their British and US allies as they were of their enemies, so their facilities had to be brought with them. Arctic convoys relied on their own bases in Iceland and Britain, with minimal support received from the Soviets once they arrived in Russian ports.

In 1942 all Russian-bound convoys originated from either Iceland (Reykjavík or the adjacent Hvalfjörður), or from Britain in either Scotland (Loch Ewe or Oban) or Lancashire (Liverpool). Homebound convoys returned to Reykjavík or Loch Ewe through 1944; but in 1941 convoys arrived at Kirkwall or Scapa Flow, and in 1945 convoys arrived at the Firth of Clyde, all in Scotland.

Between departure and arrival, convoys were almost entirely dependent upon their own resources. Coastal Command aircraft lacked the range to patrol much further north than the middle of the Norwegian Sea, and only a few hundred miles east of Iceland, and the Soviets ignored requests to provide air escort north of the Kola Peninsula or even in the White Sea. The few air assets Coastal Command had stationed in Russia focused on tracking and attacking Kriegsmarine surface warships. Even had they been available, the Hampdens and Catalinas in Russia were unsuitable for defending convoys against their main threat, Luftwaffe aircraft. This did not mean however that convoys were without resources, rather, they simply depended on what they brought with them.

In 1942, Arctic convoys consisted of eight to 40 merchant ships, with convoy sizes increasing through September 1942. Earlier convoys consisted of eight to ten cargo ships,

while PQ-18, sent in September had 40. Merchant ships in Arctic convoys tended to be newer and faster than the typical cargo vessels in the Atlantic theatre, as Arctic conditions demanded well-found ships. They were carrying high-priority cargoes (aircraft, weapons, ammunition and fuel), and needed to make ten knots to keep up with the convoy.

Murmansk in 1940. Northern Russia's only year-round ice-free harbour was close to the German lines and in 1941 its only rail connection ran to Leningrad, which soon fell under siege. (AC)

The ships used were break-bulk freighters, typical of the era, carrying between 2,500 and 10,000 deadweight tons of cargo. While a wide variety of ships were used, the bulk fell into one of three broad categories: Hog Islanders, Empire, Fort and Ocean vessels, and Liberty Ships. Hog Islanders were the collective name for ships built by the US Emergency Fleet Corporation for service in World War I. Most were completed after the war ended, and they dominated the roles of the world's freighter lines in the between-war years.

Empire, Fort and Ocean ships were vessels ordered by and built for Britain's Ministry of War Transport to expand the British mercantile fleet during World War II and replace war losses. All three classes were built to a standard design. The ships all contained the word 'Empire,' 'Fort' or 'Ocean,' in their name with the word indicating where they were built. 'Empire' ships being built in Great Britain, 'Fort' vessels in Canada and 'Ocean' ships in the United States.

The Liberty Ship was an adaptation of the 'Ocean' design. It was mass produced in the United States, with 2,710 built between 1941 and 1945. While pre-war construction predominated in the early Arctic convoys, by 1942 war-construction vessels were increasing.

Cargoes were loaded in either the United Kingdom or the United States, and ships generally returned in ballast, although occasionally raw materials (typically timber) were carried west. Ships were sent to the departure point where they awaited assembly of the full convoy, and only after both merchantmen and escort was ready, would the convoy sail. Sometimes ships waited months in port before departing and a round trip could take as long as a year.

Arctic convoys were heavily escorted, and it was not unusual for convoys to have more escort warships than merchantmen. The escort always included antisubmarine warfare vessels to protect against U-boats, and cruisers often accompanied the close escort if a Kriegsmarine sortie was feared. A distant escort including fleet aircraft carriers, battleships and heavy cruisers accompanied convoys when intelligence indicated heavy surface units, battleships, battlecruisers and *panzershiff* (commonly called 'pocket battleships'), too heavy for the close escorts to fight successfully were likely to be present.

This distant escort remained well out of range of Luftwaffe aircraft, as these posed as great a threat to Allied warships as they did to merchantmen. They also never ventured

British Fort, Empire or Ocean types of freighters (shown) were wartime constructions which were mass-produced. The Liberty ship's design was taken from these ships. These classes of freighters formed the backbone of ships filling Arctic convoys. (AC)

Antisubmarine trawlers (such as the one shown) and motor minesweepers were always important parts of Arctic convoy escorts. In addition to their ASW role and occasional use for towing, these tough little craft could prove surprisingly effective against Luftwaffe aircraft. (AC)

too far east. The lack of repair facilities for major warships in Russia meant damage repairable under normal circumstances could be fatal to a British warship stranded, damaged, in Russian waters. Two large cruisers, *Edinburgh* and *Trinidad* were lost in the Arctic to damage this way, scuttled after being damaged and disabled under circumstances where they might have been salvaged had they been closer to Allied ports.

As convoys grew larger, auxiliary ships were added to the escort, to provide infrastructure and facilities missing in the Arctic. These included oilers, rescue ships and salvage vessels, which were always Royal Fleet Auxiliaries. A civilian branch of the Royal Navy, RNA ships were manned by civilians wearing Royal Navy uniforms and under naval discipline. RNA vessels flew a Blue Ensign (Union Jack in the upper canton, on a blue field) to distinguish them from British warships or ordinary commercial vessels – Royal Navy warships flew the White Ensign (Union Jack in the canton, on a white field with a red cross of St George quartering the field), while British-flagged merchant vessels flew the Red Duster (Union Jack in the canton, on a red field).

An oiler was a tanker capable of refuelling ships at sea, which carried bunker oil in its tanks. This increased the endurance of the small vessels attached to the close escorts, especially the fuel-hungry destroyers. They could also provide return-trip fuel for oil-burning convoy vessels, as supplies in Russia were frequently short. Furthermore, surplus fuel unneeded for the return trip could be unloaded in Russia as additional cargo.

Rescue ships were vessels designated to recover survivors from ships sunk during the convoy's transit. In the freezing Arctic waters, the life of an immersed man, even when wearing protective clothing, was measured in minutes. Men in open boats or rafts would die of exposure within days, even in the Arctic summer, and survival was measured in hours during winter months. Immediate rescue was therefore required. The rescue ships were typically small freighters with passenger cabins, converted to rescue duties. Passenger accommodation was increased, and galley and food storage capabilities enlarged. Converted from quick and manoeuvrable merchant vessels, they were armed, carried cargo and were generally stationed at the rear of the convoy to facilitate rescue activities.

Salvage ships were tasked with recovering vessels damaged en route. Generally drawn from the antisubmarine trawlers assigned to the close escort, these were capable of towing a ship at convoy speeds. Salvage was rarely attempted during 1942, however, on rare occasions it could be attempted. Furthermore it was better to have the capability on hand, especially since trawlers added to the convoy's ASW capability.

Often damage meant a ship under tow could not keep up with the convoy. The risks associated with towing crippled ships usually outweighed their value, or its cargo's value, even when it could stay in the convoy. Independently, with only a tow ship for protection, the risk to both ships became suicidal and, in those instances, the crew was taken off the damaged ship, which was then scuttled.

Regardless of season, convoys kept close to the edge of the polar ice cap. In the summer, when it receded north, the Luftwaffe was out in force and so the further north the convoy sailed the less exposure it had to enemy aircraft. In the winter, when the ice pack moved south, convoys still preferred to maximize their distance from German-held coasts.

Weapons and tactics

The chief weapon and tactic used during the Arctic campaign by the Western Allies was the convoy itself. While not often thought of as such, the twentieth-century convoy was both.

Convoys were used for centuries to protect lightly armed merchant vessels from marauding enemies, whether pirates, privateers or national warships. The escort was generally made up of smaller warships, frigates and sloops-of-war in the sailing era. While vastly outnumbered by the convoyed ships, the escorts were usually strong enough to drive off any single marauder. Convoying increased the risks to raiders attempting to capture prizes, and limited the number of vessels captured if raids succeeded.

Steam power and radio however reduced convoy usefulness. Steam liberated ships from dependence on wind, while simultaneously limiting a ship's endurance – steam engines ate fuel and the amount of fuel used grew exponentially as speed increased. For surface raiders, endurance shrank from months to a week or two. Lone raiders, unsupported by a fleet, were soon run down by the enemy's cruisers, especially once radio appeared, and it could be tracked by radio reports when it attacked. By the start of the 1904 Russo-Japanese War, convoys were largely abandoned except very near enemy coasts.

The submarine's appearance in World War I revived the convoy. Submarines were largely invisible, and deadly against independently sailing unarmed merchantmen. They were extremely fragile but, unlike expensive cruisers, they were cheap and disposable, and they made commerce raiding viable again. The convoy countered the World War I submarine. Keeping ships in convoy eliminated most opportunities for U-boats to find targets and, when they did, armed merchantmen made it too risky for a U-boat to attack with its deck gun, then the favoured tactic due to limited torpedoes. Some 40 to 50 ships firing at a surfaced U-boat meant chances of a hit were high, and if the convoy got lucky just once, the Kaiser would be minus a U-boat. Throw in naval warships as escorts, and U-boats became completely ineffective against ships in convoys.

World War II added two fresh factors: wolf-pack tactics and aircraft. The wolf pack, multiple U-boats making

The quick-firing 2-pdr 'Pom-Pom' gun was Britain's primary light antiaircraft gun when World War II began. It fired a 40mm round, and was mounted on British warships, from battleships to armed trawlers. Its main failing was there were too few of them. (AC)

OPPOSITE DEFENDING AN ARCTIC CONVOY WITH ANTIAIRCRAFT ARTILLERY

Although the real defence from attacking aircraft came from effective carrier-based fighters, vigorous, coordinated antiaircraft artillery aggressively deployed significantly reduced the threat aircraft posed to convoys. PQ-17 successfully neutralized the Luftwaffe prior to dispersion, and PQ-18's antiaircraft fire generally deterred attacking aircraft. This plate shows how antiaircraft fire defended convoys.

coordinated attacks, negated some of the convoy's strengths. They carried enough torpedoes to devastate a convoy without using deck guns, and could split the attention of the convoy escort with fresh U-boats attacking a convoy while the escorts were attacking the previous U-boats that had attacked.

Aircraft were an even greater threat, especially massed aircraft attacks. Merchant ships were slow, unwieldy targets, and though early in the war they were armed to fight U-boats, their antiaircraft armament was minimal. Even most pre-war warships had antiaircraft batteries incapable of dealing with the fast metal monoplanes of 1939 and later.

Aircraft stripped the convoy of one of its chief advantages. Concentrating merchant shipping in one location made all merchant ships more difficult to find – U-boats had a search horizon of only three or four miles, and cruisers could spot targets 15 miles away, so at surface speed it took a lot of U-boats or cruisers sweeping a lot of sea to find a convoy. But, at patrol aircraft cruising speeds (150–250mph), with an effective radius of 20 miles, a maritime patrol aircraft could cover a lot of ocean. Once spotted by aircraft, slow-moving convoys had difficulty breaking contact and could not move fast enough to evade subsequent patrols. The patrolling aircraft then guided U-boats, surface warships and other aircraft to the convoy.

Even then, the convoy remained the best method of moving large amounts of cargo across disputed seas. The Fw 200 proved how vulnerable independently sailing merchantmen were to armed aircraft, even improvised warplanes like the Condor. A convoy at least concentrated defensive capabilities.

A convoy's primary protection against aircraft were the antiaircraft guns carried aboard both warships and merchantmen. Heavy guns ranged from a 3in to a 5.25in bore. The lightest, the 3in gun fired a 12lb projectile up to 4 miles. By 1942, these were largely mounted on merchant vessels. The 5in gun, generally the 5in/38 US dual-purpose gun, fired a 55lb projectile. It fired 15 rounds per minute, with a 37,200ft ceiling and could reach low-flying aircraft up to 8.5 miles away.

British destroyers, cruisers, antiaircraft ships and some merchantmen carried a variety of 4in, 4.5in and 4.7in antiaircraft guns. The 4in, a standard antiaircraft gun on British pre-war cruisers, fired a 31lb shell, with a 28,000ft ceiling and 6.6-mile effective range. The 4.5in fired a 55lb shell, with a 29,910ft ceiling and a 9.6-mile effective range. The 4.7in was primarily a surface weapon, with limited antiaircraft capability since it had separate propellant and charge which made it less effective as an antiaircraft weapon. It fired a 50lb projectile, with a range of 8.5 miles and a ceiling of 21,000ft.

Ships were also equipped with a wide array of light antiaircraft guns: rifle calibre Lewis guns, 50 calibre machine guns, pom-poms, 1.1in guns, 20mm Oerlikons and 40mm Bofors. The most effective was the Bofors, followed by the Oerlikon, though these were in short supply in 1942 (although the situation eased as the year progressed). They fired 2lb and 0.27lb projectiles respectively; the Bofors was deadly within 15,000ft, while the Oerlikon was best used within 4,000ft.

Antiaircraft fire was largely aimed visually at this stage of the war, and radar-controlled fire lay in the future. Antiaircraft fire was often laid and aimed locally, which further reduced effectiveness, and gun crews aboard merchantmen were rarely highly trained, occasionally being more dangerous to other ships in the convoy than

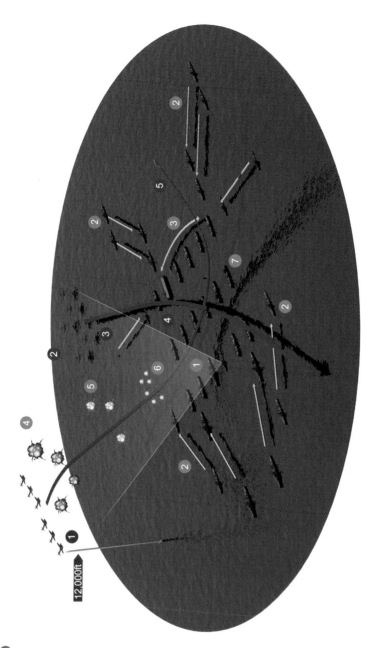

British Forces

1 Incoming enemy aircraft are spotted on radar.
2 Destroyers move to antiaircraft positions.
3 Carrier (if present) moves to station away from incoming aircraft.
4 Heavy AA guns (4.5in, 4in etc) open fire as aircraft come into range.
5 Medium AA (40mm, pom-poms open fire).
6 Light AA (20mm and smaller) open fire.
7 If necessary, AA ships shift to protect endangered ship(s).

German Forces ●

1 Incoming Ju 88 spotted on radar at 12,000ft.
2 Incoming torpedo bombers are timed to attack minutes after the level bombers.
3 Torpedo bombers at 200ft spotted by radar.
4 Level bombers attack convoy.
5 Torpedo bombers attack convoy.

Merchant vessels were armed with a wide array of guns, from the US 5in/38 antiaircraft gun on Liberty Ships to 0.50cal and 0.30cal machine guns. This shows a pair of guns aboard a British merchantman, most likely a 4in gun (right) for use against U-boats, and a 2-pdr antiaircraft gun (left). (AC)

enemy aircraft.

The best way to defeat attacking aircraft was with other aircraft. In the Atlantic even four-engine long-range patrol aircraft, such as the Liberator or Sunderland, could break up air attacks against convoys, but the Arctic route took convoys out of range of land-based Allied aircraft. The alternative was to take ship-based aircraft with the convoy.

Ideal were escort carriers, aircraft carriers built on a merchant hull. They typically made only 20 knots, but that was fast enough to keep up with a convoy. HMS *Audacity*, the first such conversion used for convoy escort, proved the concept dramatically when, in late 1941, it escorted four convoys between Britain and Gibraltar, successfully driving both U-boats and aircraft away from the convoy, before being sunk in December 1941.

As 1942 started, Britain and the United States were desperately short of escort carriers. They took much less time to build than 30-knot fleet carriers, but until *Audacity* proved the concept, few resources were committed to building them. The first production escort carriers were only just coming into service in 1942, and not until September was one allocated to cover an Arctic convoy.

Even then, there was a critical shortage of carrier aircraft as the RAF had neglected to build naval aircraft during the inter-war period. While the Fleet Air Arm resumed control of carrier aircraft in 1939, even by 1942 they lacked both trained aircrew and carrier aircraft enough to provide full air groups for their fleet carriers, much less escort carriers. The one escort carrier assigned an Arctic convoy had an air group of only nine aircraft: six Hurricanes and three Swordfish.

To augment escort carriers, Britain used Catapult Armed Merchantmen or CAM ships. These were conventional merchant ships outfitted with a catapult, which could launch one aircraft. Once launched, the aircraft had to either ditch or fly to a land base when the mission ended. Alternatively, the pilot could bail out, though whether ditching or bailing out, the pilot's survival depended upon being recovered from Arctic waters before freezing. Typically there was only one CAM in a convoy, and they carried only one aircraft which, since they were disposable, were usually those at the end of their service life. It was like protecting a stagecoach from a pack of highwaymen with a one-shot blunderbuss. Despite this, CAM ships proved their utility on four Arctic convoys.

CAMPAIGN OBJECTIVES
Norway and Russia

German objectives and plans

The most important consideration in discussing German actions against Allied Arctic convoys was that the Wehrmacht, Kriegsmarine and Luftwaffe resources in Norway and Finland were not there to attack convoys. The Kriegsmarine and Luftwaffe were in Norway to repel an Anglo-American invasion of the country, and the Wehrmacht in Norway had the same responsibility. Axis ground forces in Finland had the additional strategic objective of capturing the Soviet-held portions of the Kola Peninsula.

On 26 and 27 December 1941, British Commandos launched two raids on Norway: Operation *Anklet* and Operation *Archery*. *Anklet* was a 300-man raid of the Lofoten Islands in which a combined arms assault saw two radio transmitters destroyed, several ships captured or sunk, and 200 Germans and Quislings taken prisoner. Furthermore, about 200 Norwegians left the islands to serve in the Free Norwegian armed forces. *Archery* was a larger (570 men) but similar raid of the town of Måløy on South Vågsøy Island, roughly halfway between Bergen and Trondheim. Its goal was the destruction of the fish oil factories and storage tanks at Måløy. Nearly 100 German defenders were captured, another 120 killed and 70 Norwegians returned with the British to join Free Norwegian forces.

Both were pinprick raids, intended to rattle and distract the Germans. That goal succeeded beyond its planners' wildest expectations and the German high command (OKW) immediately ordered the Kriegsmarine to send five extra U-boats north. This raised the U-boats available to fight Arctic convoys to nine, double the number in 1941. However, since those boats were diverted from their original destination of the American Atlantic coast, that was a net gain. There were fewer ships crossing the Arctic than moving along the American east coast, so U-boats in the Arctic had fewer targets.

The twin raids also convinced Hitler an invasion of Norway was imminent. The British had no such plans, but willingly fostered his belief. Every German soldier sent to Norway was a soldier unavailable to fight in Russia or North Africa, and Hitler ordered the equivalent of an army corps, 30,000 solders, to reinforce the Wehrmacht's Norwegian garrison.

Tromsø was another harbour in northern Norway used by the Kriegsmarine as an anchorage. It was used to support Kriegsmarine surface warships during the Arctic campaign. (USNHHC)

A British landing party at work during the Lofoten raid. Raids on Vågsoy Island and the Lofoten Islands drew Hitler's attention to Norway and led to its reinforcement by Werhmacht, Kriegsmarine and Luftwaffe forces. (AC)

Dönitz was conducting a tonnage war against the Allies, attempting to sink ships faster than the Allies could build them, and attacks on Arctic convoys contributed to that end. Additionally, due to harsh Arctic conditions, ships sent on the Arctic run tended to be newer than average. (AC)

So far, so good. However, Hitler became convinced Norway would become the 'Zone of Destiny' and in January ordered all operational warships of the Kriegsmarine to the Norwegian and Barents Seas to defend the country from the 'imminent' landings. The OKW also ordered another 13 U-boats to guard Norway between January and March 1942. More ominously, between January and April 1942 elements of two bomber groups, Kampfgeschwader 26 and 30, were ordered north to Norway. Their He 111s and Ju 88s swelled the number of Luftwaffe aircraft in Norway, supplementing the relative handful of Fw 200s, He 115s and BV 138s already there.

The objective of these ships and aircraft was to defend Norway. However, no competent commander lets units stand idle if there are targets at hand and, in this case, the biggest and most tempting target available was the Allied Arctic convoys.

The Germans had additional factors encouraging attacks on the convoys. One was that attacking the convoys did not distract from the primary objective of defending Norway. Surface warships, U-boats and especially aircraft could attack a convoy one day, and repel an invasion on the next. It took a day for surface warships to steam from Trondheim or Bergen in central Norway to Alta Fjord or Vest Fjord on Norway's Arctic coast or vice versa. Similarly, it was a six-hour flight from Banak to Stavanger at opposite ends of Norway.

A second factor was using combat forces in battle which was preferable to having them stand idle. While practice missions and exercises were preferable to keeping men and equipment idle, an opportunity for actual combat was better still. Any fuel and munitions expended directly served the war effort, and combat better prepared men for future fighting than drills. Attacking supply convoys was directly analogous to attacking an invasion fleet.

It was more than just good practice, however. The convoys were important strategic targets. Nazi Germany was locked in a major struggle with the Soviet Union and the 1941 offensive had gone less well than planned. Russia was still in the war, as yet undefeated when 1942 began, and the aircraft, armour, weapons and ammunition being carried there by Allied convoys helped keep the Soviets fighting. Every ship sunk before it arrived deprived Russia of resources needed to stay in the war.

Every ship sunk, empty or full, was also one less ship available to carry goods for the Allies. Admiral Karl Dönitz, who commanded the Kriegsmarine's U-boats, was attempting to starve Britain by sinking more ships than the Allies could build, and Britain depended on those ships to keep it in the war. It could not feed its people or its war industries without a steady supply of resources brought to Britain aboard the Allied cargo fleets. Sink enough ships, and Britain had to surrender. Sinking

ships on the Arctic run contributed to victory in Dönitz's tonnage war, and it didn't matter what sank the ships, U-boats, surface warships or aircraft.

It did, however, matter to the Luftwaffe. While the Luftwaffe was fighting foreign enemies in 1941 and 1942, the opponents it most desired to triumph over were its rival services, the Wehrmacht and the Kriegsmarine. Interservice rivalries were real and fierce in Nazi Germany, and were encouraged by Hitler who permitted development of three independent land armies (the Wehrmacht, Waffen SS and Luftwaffe Land Army) and fostered rivalry between all branches of the German military.

This was done to forestall a military coup. Preservation of the Nazi Reich was Hitler's primary objective, and this way no one branch of the military had sufficient power to independently topple the Nazi government. The Wehrmacht was held in check by the independent ground forces and the Luftwaffe and the Kriegsmarine. Similarly, the Luftwaffe or Kriegsmarine independently attempting a putsch would be quickly crushed. Ensuring the services mistrusted each other enough that they would never cooperate in a takeover was more important than smooth battlefield coordination.

Despite this photo's apparent amity between Hitler and Goering, the Nazi regime was filled with violent rivalries. This was encouraged by Hitler to reduce the chances of different services coordinating to conduct a coup. (AC)

While the Luftwaffe was involved in the Atlantic tonnage war, its participation was peripheral, limited to attacks by Kampfgeschwader 40's Fw 200s. It had dominated the eastern Mediterranean during the 1941 Balkans campaign and its aftermath, but since then the bulk of the Luftwaffe had been committed to Operation *Barbarossa*, the Nazi invasion of Russia.

Now though it had bombers available in Norway, required to remain there by orders of the Fuhrer himself. Arctic convoys, targets worthy of the Luftwaffe's attention, came within range every month or so and it was more than just an opportunity to injure the British and Russians. The Luftwaffe had an opportunity to show it could do what the Kriegsmarine's U-boats and warships had failed thus far to do: stop the Arctic convoys. It was an opportunity to put one in the eye of the Kriegsmarine, and show how much more effective aircraft were than ships or U-boats at playing the tonnage war.

There was little in the way of long-range strategic planning against convoys, however, and certainly little in the way of interservice cooperation. The Luftwaffe and Kriegsmarine ran independent wars against the convoys: the Luftwaffe only grudgingly gave aerial reconnaissance information to the Kriegsmarine and the Kriegsmarine rarely received air cover, even within range of Luftwaffe fighters. Like two rival tribes battling a common foe, the two branches competed to see who could collect the most kills without involving the other.

Luftwaffe planning remained largely operational. When the Luftwaffe received indications a convoy was expected, they shifted available aircraft to northern airfields and air patrols were increased. Once the convoy was spotted its route was plotted, and bomber strikes sent after it.

What central planning existed tended to be top-down, impulsive and poorly considered. To cite one example, when Herman Goering learned Convoy PQ-18 had an escort carrier accompanying it, he sent pre-emptive orders for the carrier to be sunk first, before attacking other ships in the convoy. The day previous to the order being sent, eight merchantmen were torpedoed and sunk by Luftwaffe aircraft. The next day, pursuing new orders, bombers ignored several easy opportunities to sink merchantmen to attack the carrier at the other end of the convoy. The aircraft took heavy casualties from antiaircraft fire, but failed to damage the carrier.

The Luftwaffe had it easier than the surface ships of the Kriegsmarine, when it came to planning. Hitler was terrified of losing surface warships, especially battleships, but his fears extended down to destroyers. Any attempts to attack convoys with Kriegsmarine capital ships were hedged with restrictions to prevent their loss. Their freedom of action was so circumscribed as to make them ineffectual. When they failed – something virtually inevitable given their operational restrictions – Hitler would then castigate the Kriegsmarine over its ineffectiveness and lack of aggression.

Allied objectives and plans

The objective of the Western Allies, Great Britain, the Commonwealth Nations and the United States, was simple. Get the maximum tonnage of military cargoes to Russia via the Arctic route at a minimum loss of cargo and ships. As with many simple things, it was not easy.

Through spring 1941 Britain and its Commonwealth had been fighting the Axis powers virtually alone. Their only allies were a collection of governments-in-exile from countries conquered by the Axis and the friendly neutrality of the United States. Until the Soviets entered the war, Britain seemed on a slow path to defeat. However, when Hitler invaded the Soviet Union in June 1941, he gave beleaguered Britain the gift of a powerful ally. While the Nazi war machine marched through much of the Soviet Union's western territories in the summer of 1941, the sheer size of Russia kept it from being defeated in the fashion of Germany's earlier conquests.

Winston Churchill despised Communism and had been an implacable foe of the Soviet Union since its inception. Regardless, he realized the opportunity an alliance with the hated Soviets offered and, despite his antipathy for the Communist regime, was willing to aid them, stating, 'If Hitler invaded hell I would make at least a favourable reference to the devil in the House of Commons.'

In the Russian campaign's opening month the Soviets were short of everything but invaders. Most of their aircraft, tanks and artillery pieces were destroyed in the opening weeks, and replacement was constrained as the Nazis and their Axis allies overran the

Sir Stafford Cripps, British ambassador to the Soviet Union, signs the Anglo-Soviet Agreement on behalf of Great Britain on 12 July 1941 in Moscow. Stalin stands directly behind Sir Stafford. This alliance gave rise to Arctic convoys. (AC)

manufacturing centres in the western Soviet Union. In many cases the Soviets moved the factories' equipment east to the Ural Mountains and beyond, but those factories would not resume partial production for many months and full production for up to a year.

Keeping the Soviet Union in the war was a critical priority for Churchill. Unless the Soviets received weapons to continue in the war, they might be forced to surrender; Churchill broadcast a promise of aid the night the Axis invaded. In pursuit of this goal the British Commonwealth and Soviet Union signed an Anglo-Soviet Agreement on 12 July 1941. In it both powers agreed to fight together and not make a separate peace, and Churchill agreed to send military supplies, especially tanks and warplanes, to Russia.

In August, Churchill dispatched a convoy of seven cargo ships and the aircraft carrier *Argus* to Arkhangelsk. Known as Dervish, it was the first of what became 78 convoys which took the Arctic route before the European war ended in May 1945. This convoy was sent over the objection of Britain's First Sea Lord, Admiral Dudley Pound, who felt the effort foolhardy. The route took ships well past British air cover and close to the northern coast of German-occupied Norway, where airfields and anchorages gave the Luftwaffe and Kriegsmarine easy access to British convoys from nearby bases.

Politics dictated the Arctic route be used. The materiel brought to Russia in Arctic convoys was needed badly and immediately, and there was no faster way to get it there. The first set of fighters and tanks delivered to Russia helped defend the ports at which they landed.

Furthermore, they were as important politically as militarily. Despite the Anglo-Soviet Agreement, one of Churchill's greatest fears was that the Soviet Union would arrange a separate peace with the Nazis. Nor were Churchill's fears unreasonable. In the weeks following the German invasion, even as the Anglo-Soviet Agreement was being negotiated and signed, Stalin was conducting back-channel negotiations with Germany. He offered Hitler the Ukraine and all of the Soviet Union west of the Ukraine in exchange for peace. Fortunately for Churchill, Hitler ignored the request, believing he would soon conquer all of the Soviet Union. These negotiations were kept secret long after the war ended, but Churchill

By December 1941 the Germans were at Moscow. A resolute Soviet defence kept the Germans from capturing the Russian capital but the offensive underscored the Soviet's need for more aid from the west, and the necessity for more and larger Arctic convoys. (AC)

ARMS FOR RUSSIA . . . A great convoy of British ships escorted by Soviet fighter planes sails into Murmansk harbour with vital supplies for the Red Army.

A British propaganda poster showing an Arctic convoy arriving in Murmansk. An uncharacteristic show of Soviet air cover is portrayed, along with antiaircraft fire downing a German bomber. This was the ideal, not the reality. (Wikimedia Commons)

did not need to hear of them to believe it possible. No leader, including Hitler, was as cynical and self-serving as Stalin.

As the war progressed the need for convoys increased, even after the United States entered the conflict. Stalin made them part of the price for continued Soviet participation. While Hitler was stopped at the gates of Moscow in December 1941, Russia was still on the defensive and, after the Axis renewed their offensive in spring 1942, the Soviet situation grew more desperate as the Germans pushed deep into the Southern Russian steppes and into the oil-producing region of the Caucasus.

All the while Stalin berated his Anglo-American allies for the lack of supplies. Casualties among convoy ships and escorts failed to impress him since they were miniscule compared to Soviet losses in the land war. Instead, Stalin stoked the Western Allies' fears that the Soviets might be defeated unless adequate support was received.

As a result, and over Admiralty objections, Churchill insisted the convoys be continued and the number of cargo ships sent increased over the course of 1942. Churchill also wanted the number of convoys increased as well, with the ships sailing on a ten-day cadence instead of the monthly sailings maintained previously. The lack of escorts and cargo ships however prevented that. Even so, inadequate port facilities meant cargoes sent often piled up on wharves and ships remained in port, unable to unload.

As it was, sending a monthly convoy strained the resources of the Royal Navy who had responsibility for planning and executing them. Through most of 1942, with the sole exception of July's PQ-17/QP-14 sailings, all warships involved were Royal Navy ships. Eastbound convoys were labelled PQ convoys (the initials coming from the initial of the Royal Navy officer organizing the convoys, Commander Phillip Quellyn Roberts). Westbound convoys flipped the initials: QP. By 1942 convoy departures were coordinated with the homeward-bound QP convoys, typically sailing on or up to a week after the PQ convoy left port. This was done in order to split the Germans' attention between the two convoys, and it generally worked. German attacks normally focused on only one of the two convoys in every cycle.

It also optimized the use of escorts as every convoy was protected by several sets of escorts. There was always a 'through' set of close escorts, which remained with the convoy throughout the voyage, protecting the convoy. The 'through' escorts accompanying a PQ convoy formed the core of the through escort of the subsequent QP convoy. There was often a heavier covering force of close escorts intended to provide close protection outbound to Russia through what was considered the most hazardous portion of the voyage. These vessels then broke off to cover the homeward-bound QP convoy. Finally, there was a heavy covering force including battleships and aircraft carriers intended to protect the convoy from German heavy surface warships.

At the Russian end of the voyage, the convoys were guarded by Russian escorts. These accompanied the homebound QP convoys over the initial leg of the departure and were supposed to join the Russian-bound PQ convoys near where the British escort broke off. Generally though they only covered the portion of the voyage near the approach to Murmansk and in the White Sea.

The exact mix of escorts depended on the threat offered to the convoy. The Germans could attack a convoy in one of four ways: by using U-boats, light surface ships like destroyers, heavy surface ships such as battleships or aircraft. Each threat had a different offsetting defence.

The through escort was primarily an anti-U-boat force, and this was the main threat against which it protected convoys. It contained ships such as antisubmarine trawlers, corvettes and escort destroyers. In a pinch, the trawlers did double duty as tugs, while the corvettes acted as rescue ships.

The covering force close escorts were primarily intended to protect convoys from light surface warships, especially German destroyers. They consisted of light cruisers and fleet destroyers, capable of defeating enemy destroyers. At need they could, and did, battle heavier units such as German heavy cruisers and *Panzerschiffe*. While these sometimes continued through to Russia, they often returned independently of the convoy they escorted.

The distant escort was viewed primarily as protection from German capital ships. They were dispatched only if Kriegsmarine heavy units were believed ready for sea – while the Royal Navy did not know whether the heavy warships were actually at sea or where they were if they left port, signal and photographic intelligence warned when they were ready to set sail.

But what did plans call for in dealing with aircraft? Initially, nothing other than the antiaircraft guns of the escorting warships and convoyed ships. While the route took ships within range of Luftwaffe bombers, the Admiralty's biggest concern initially were Kriegsmarine capital ships, destroyers and U-boats, in that order. By far the biggest concern were the German battleships and battlecruisers; the Admiralty worried over these to the point of obsession. Antiaircraft defences took fourth priority, and a distant fourth at that.

Throughout the critical year of 1942 Britain added further antiaircraft protection to Arctic convoys, initially adding a CAM ship or two to deal with reconnaissance aircraft. As the threat became clearer, antiaircraft cruisers were added to convoys, and, finally, at the end an escort carrier. But antiaircraft planning was always too little – and generally one step behind German planning.

A new supply route opened in 1942 with the Anglo-Soviet occupation of Iran. It ran from the Persian Gulf port of Abadan (shown), through Iran by rail to the Caspian Sea and thence to Russia. It was slower, but more secure, and did not reach its capacity until after the crisis year of 1942. (AC)

THE CAMPAIGN
Battleground in the far north

Convoy PQ-15 was the first convoy to include a CAM ship. The ship, *Empire Morn*, carried a catapult-launched Sea Hurricane, or 'Hurricat', and provided a small measure of air cover for the convoy. (SDA&SM)

Arctic convoys travelled to Russia from August 1941 until May 1945. The first convoy, code-named Dervish, departed Hvalfjörður, Iceland, on 21 August 1941. The final one, RA-67, closed the series arriving in Clyde on 30 May 1945, 23 days after Germany formally surrendered and 22 days short of four years after Nazi Germany invaded the Soviet Union.

During the four-years the convoys ran, the Arctic run gained a reputation as the most hazardous convoy route of the Atlantic theatre – a reputation that was merited. On a percentage basis the Arctic convoys had a higher loss rate than any other regularly scheduled convoys in the European theatre, and only the irregular Malta convoys suffered greater losses.

That reputation was gained during just one year, 1942. It was the first year Germany seriously opposed the Arctic convoys and was also the only year Germany brought the full force of the Luftwaffe against the Arctic convoys. As 1942 progressed, both sides raised the stakes, with the Allies increasing the size of their convoys and massively increasing the surface escort they provided, and with the Luftwaffe increasing the number of aircraft they used against the convoys, the variety of weapons and improving tactics.

As 1942 advanced the Luftwaffe made itself felt and Allied casualties kept mounting. They had devastated the Royal Navy in the eastern Mediterranean early in 1942, and when they turned their attention to the Arctic they proved as devastating to ships in a convoy. Britain attempted to counter the Luftwaffe's threat as 1942 continued with increased antiaircraft protection. However, Britain lacked the one tool most effective against Luftwaffe aircraft – sufficient aircraft of their own to oppose them. Neither CAM fighters nor carrier aircraft were available early enough or present in sufficient numbers when they arrived. Therein lay the real story of the Arctic run's violent reputation.

Origins: 21 August 1941–22 February 1942

On 21 August 1941 six merchant vessels accompanied by an oiler and escorted by nine warships departed Hvalfjörður. Five of the cargo ships flew the Red Duster; one was Dutch and all were elderly. The largest and oldest, the 11,348grt *Llanstephan Castle* was launched in 1914, whereas the newest, the 4,747grt *New Westminster City*, entered service in 1929.

While the ships were not noteworthy, their destination was: the northern Russian port city of Arkhangelsk. Established in the late sixteenth century, the city was Russia's oldest northern port. It began as a timber port, exporting lumber to Britain, and was still largely a timber port when World War II began, with a rail link to Moscow. Nestled on the White Sea, it was icebound during the northern winter, approachable only though paths cut by icebreakers in the spring and autumn. Yet its railroad link meant supplies unloaded at Arkhangelsk could be sent to Russian battlefields or Soviet factories as needed.

The only other northern Russian ports with a rail link to inland Russia were the ports of Polyarnoe and Murmansk, located on opposite sides of Kola Bay. On the Murman coast of the Kola Peninsula, they were much newer than Archangelsk. Polyarnoe was established in 1898 and Murmansk in 1916. Their big advantage over the older port was that they remained ice-free year-round. The railroad had been built to rush war supplies unloaded at Murmansk to St Petersburg during World War I.

In August 1941 Arkhangelsk had an edge over its Murman rival. The front line was only 15 miles from Murmansk, and Leningrad (as St Petersburg was renamed after the Russian Revolution) was newly besieged by the Axis. It was not then clear that the Soviets could keep the Axis from capturing Murmansk and, additionally, until a new railroad linking to Arkhangelsk's Moscow line was completed in autumn 1941 what landed at Murmansk, stayed in Murmansk. Through December of that year Arkhangelsk would remain the port of destination for Britain's Arctic convoys.

The six ships were part of a convoy code-named 'Dervish', hastily assembled to send cargoes needed by Great Britain's newest ally, the Soviet Union. The ships chosen were those available, and they carried cargoes of rubber, tin and wool, raw materials desperately needed by Soviet factories. They also carried 15 crated Hawker Hurricane fighters. Dervish arrived in Arkhangelsk on 31 August.

The day before Dervish arrived, HMS *Argus*, the Royal Navy's oldest aircraft carrier, along with heavy cruiser *Shropshire* and three destroyers left port on Operation *Strength*. They carried personnel from the RAF's 151 Wing to Russia. *Argus* carried 24 Hurricanes, which were flown off to Vaenga, an airfield covering Murmansk, and the RAF personnel were landed at Murmansk, to assist the Soviets. The operation was covered by a Home Fleet force built around fleet carrier *Victorious*, two cruisers and three destroyers.

In 1941, conditions in all three Russian ports were primitive. At Arkhangelsk there were only six wharves, and these could only accommodate small ships, up to 1,000 tons. Furthermore, there were no facilities capable of carrying out major repairs, and no drydock. The oiler *Aldersdale* accompanied Dervish to provide fuel for the return trip, and three

The natural hazards of the Arctic weather were compounded by the threat of Nazi aircraft, surface warships and U-boats. It was no easier for the Germans, who faced the same Arctic conditions as their Allied opponents. (AC)

Aircraft carrier HMS *Argus*, a World War I veteran, carried the first load of Hawker Hurricanes to Russia. In Operation *Strength*, 24 Hurricanes flew off *Argus* to Vaenga, an airfield near the Murman coast. (AC)

escorting warships were minesweepers. They provided antisubmarine protection during the voyage and remained in Russia after arrival, where they could keep the approaches clear of mines.

Dervish was the first of 42 outbound convoys to Russia and 38 homeward-bound convoys from Russia via the Arctic route in World War II. While hastily arranged and improvised, it set a pattern followed later.

Churchill wanted convoys sailing to Russia once every ten days, similar to the convoy schedule in the North Atlantic. Admiralty officials convinced Churchill this was impossible, due to the heavy escort required. Dervish had a continuous escort of only three destroyers, three coal-burning antisubmarine trawlers and three minesweepers, yet it was also protected by five other escorts over at least part of the journey, including an antiaircraft cruiser. Additionally, a Home Fleet covering force went to sea in case German surface units appeared. In late 1941 the Royal Navy lacked the warships to provide a sufficiently heavy escort for a ten-day sailing schedule.

Instead, Churchill agreed to send convoys monthly. Outbound PQ convoys and inbound QP convoys were to start at roughly the same time, allowing escort resources to be maximized, and the next outbound and inbound Russian convoys constituted the first convoys in this series. The outbound ships carried cargoes on Stalin's wish list of critical resources, and the homebound ships sailed in ballast or carried timber from Arkhangelsk.

PQ-1 departed Hvalfjörður on 28 September 1941, two days short of a month after Dervish arrived at Arkhangelsk. It was better organized than Dervish with ten cargo ships, and, except for the ancient Panamanian-flagged *North King*, the ships were on average a decade newer than those hastily assembled for Dervish. They carried 50,000 tons of cargo, including 20 tanks and 193 fighters. They were escorted by a heavy cruiser, a destroyer and four ocean-going minesweepers (also destined to remain in Russia). Several other destroyers temporarily joined the escort during parts of the voyage.

Simultaneously, the six ships of Dervish, accompanied by seven Soviet cargo ships, departed Arkhangelsk. *Llanstephan Castle* carried 200 Polish airmen, formerly imprisoned by the Soviets, to join Free Polish Forces. Escorted by eight warships, including two heavy cruisers and a destroyer, they comprised convoy QP-1. The convoy would be joined en route by the outbound convoy's oiler, accompanied by another destroyer.

Both convoys arrived at their destinations without incident: Arkhangelsk on 11 October for the outbound convoy and Scapa Flow on 10 October for the homebound one. More remarkable was that both convoys were so unremarkable. The Royal Navy expected heavy opposition from the Germans, yet *Strength*, Dervish and the PQ–QP convoy pair sailed unmolested by the Axis.

British fears were premature. Dönitz was conducting his tonnage war in the target-laden grey waters of the Atlantic, the Kriegsmarine's surface units, except for a few still in French ports, were concentrated in the Baltic supporting Russian operations, and, while the Luftwaffe had plenty of aircraft, most were tied up supporting the Wehrmacht in Russia. The Axis was simply ignoring the Arctic convoys. And they continued ignoring them through to the end of December as the Russian campaign absorbed the totality of Luftwaffe and Wehrmacht attention and the German push on Moscow and the Soviet counteroffensive reached a climax.

Meanwhile, monthly PQ convoys sailed. PQ-2 departed Liverpool for Arkhangelsk with seven ships on 13 October 1941. The rest departed from Hvalfjörður for Arkhangelsk: PQ-3 with eight ships on 9 November, and PQ-4 with another eight ships on 27 November. These three convoys carried over 100,000 tons of supplies to Arkhangelsk. Three convoys departed Arkhangelsk before it finally iced over: QP-2 with 12 ships on 3 November 1941, QP-3 with ten ships on 27 November and QP-4 with 13 ships on 29 December. QP-2 and QP-3 arrived at Kirkwall, Scotland, although QP-3 dispersed before reaching port, the ships arriving independently. QP-4 sailed to Seidisfjord on Iceland's east coast before dispersing.

All six convoys journeyed without enemy interference. Weather, rather than the Axis, was the biggest challenge faced by these ships. QP-4, made an epic voyage through pack ice from Arkhangelsk to the open Barents Sea lead by two massive Soviet icebreakers.

Three more convoys departed for Russia in the final five weeks of 1941. PQ-6 sailed on 8 December, PQ-7A on 26 December and PQ-7B on New Year's Eve, 31 December. These were all small convoys. PQ-6 had six ships, PQ-7B had two and the largest, PQ-7B, had nine. (PQ-7 was broken into two parts because two ships were ready to sail before the other nine.) PQ-8, with eight ships left on 8 January 1942. All four departed Hvalfjörður to arrive at Murmansk. Britain was pushing convoys through as quickly as it could to take advantage of the perpetual dark of the Arctic night.

Murmansk seemed a good destination. By December, Arkhangelsk was frozen in, and the German advance to Murmansk had frozen in place – quite literally once the Arctic winter

Arkhangelsk was Russia's oldest port on its northern coast. When World War II started it was still chiefly a timber port with few wharves and docks. Its railroad linked it to Moscow, which meant cargoes could be rushed to the front once unloaded. (USNHHC)

began – the same 15 miles from the city as it had been in August. The fighters sent by Britain were garrisoning airfields around Murmansk and it seemed a relatively safe destination. By December, Murmansk's rail connection to Moscow was open and trains were running.

Only PQ-6 arrived before 1941 ended, docking in Murmansk on 20 December. It brought the total number of cargo ships safely arriving at Russia in 1941 to 51 (53 if the two oilers were counted). The convoys delivered 800 fighters, 400 tanks and 1400 military vehicles, all badly needed by the Soviets, as well as hundreds of tons of ammunition for the Soviet military and raw materials for Soviet industries. All arrived safely, but that was soon to change.

December 1941 saw the entry of the United States into World War II. Japan attacked Pearl Harbor, Hawaii, on Sunday 7 December and simultaneously attacked US possessions west of the International Date Line (where it was already 8 December). The US declared war on the Empire of Japan the next day. (Coincidentally, the day PQ-6 sailed.)

Germany had not been warned of Japan's impending action, nor was it obligated by treaty to declare war on the United States. Regardless, Germany and Italy did declare war on the United States on 11 December, with the United States reciprocating almost immediately. The US was the world's largest economy and, thanks to the US's 'Germany First' policy, its industrial strength would be brought to bear against Germany and Italy. The gratuitous declaration of war would have grave long-term consequences for the European Axis nations.

Concurrently, Britain launched two minor commando raids in Norway during late December. They were largely intended to provide a morale boost in Britain and in hopes of drawing Axis resources away from the African theatre where Britain was battling with Germany and Italy, or even relieve pressure on the Soviets. As discussed earlier, the raids succeeded beyond expectations and beyond desirability, as it convinced Hitler the Allies planned an invasion of Norway.

The most immediate consequence to Arctic convoys occurred in January. In December, Dönitz had finally shifted four U-boats to the Arctic to attack Russian convoys. Another five were diverted from voyages to the target-rich American Atlantic coast to defend Norwegian waters. The hastily dispatched PQ-7B fell victim to this new peril. The ships became separated in the winter weather and one of the two ships, the 5,135grt *Waziristan* got trapped in ice, was spotted and bombed by a Luftwaffe maritime patrol aircraft, and finally torpedoed and

A train on the Murmansk railroad, which the German advance on Leningrad cut in September 1941. This limited Murmansk's utility as a supply port until track linking the Murmansk railroad with the Arkhangelsk–Moscow line was completed. (LOC)

sunk by *U-134* south of Bear Island on 2 January 1942. It was the first merchant vessel lost on the Arctic run. PQ-7B was luckier however and all its ships arrived safely at Murmansk on 11 January, one before PQ-7A's surviving freighter, Panamanian-flagged *Cold Harbor*, arrived.

PQ-8 also showed the increasing danger of the Arctic run. The first convoy of 1942 departed Hvalfjörður on 8 January, and darkness spared it from detection from both probing aircraft and hunting U-boats until it was just one day from arrival. Then, on the morning of 17 January, *U-454* spotted the convoy and attacked.

It first torpedoed and sank the Soviet trawler *Eniesej* at 0632, part of the eastern escort. Some 12 hours later *U-454* hit 5,400grt *Harmatris* with two torpedoes. One was a dud, and minesweeper HMS *Speedwell*, also part of the eastern escort, was able to tow *Harmatris* to Murmansk the next day. Two hours after that, *U-454* fired a spread of torpedoes at freighter *British Pride*, missed and hit Tribal-class destroyer *Matabele*. Its magazine exploded, and *Matabele* sank taking all but two of its crew with it.

Nor was this the only hazard faced by PQ-8: the battleship *Tirpitz* was also to have been sent hunting the convoy but a shortage of bunker oil kept it in port. Those reports delayed the sailing of PQ-9 in mid-January. Instead, it was combined with the scheduled PQ-10, and the combined convoy sailed from Hvalfjörður on 1 February. Hidden by continuous darkness, it arrived undetected and unmolested at Murmansk on 10 February.

Convoy PQ-11 enjoyed the same good fortune, arriving at Murmansk with 13 merchantmen on 22 February. Three homeward convoys, QP-5 with four ships, QP-6 with six and QP-7 with eight departed Murmansk in January and February. All completed their voyages without incident and without loss. They would be the last undisturbed Arctic convoys for a long time.

The Tribal-class destroyer HMS *Matabele* was the first ship sunk on the Arctic run. On 17 January 1942 it was hit by a torpedo intended for the British freighter *British Pride*. It was a grim opening to 1942. (AC)

Enter the Luftwaffe: 23 February–20 April 1942

As PQ-12 assembled in Reykjavík, just south of Hvalfjörður, in late February 1942, several things had changed on the Arctic run. The first was that winter was beginning to retreat – the perpetual twilight of January and early February was broken by periods of daylight around noon, and full daylight would return quickly. By the vernal equinox the sun would be above the horizon for half the day and before May ended perpetual night would be replaced by perpetual day. Winter storms would begin to recede and the ice pack edge shift north.

The return of fair weather and daylight tended to work against convoys. Storms dispersed convoys, and darkness made it hard to keep convoys together, but they also kept the Germans at bay as the darkness concealed convoys from hunting U-boats and aircraft. Winter storms also made it difficult for U-boats to attack and kept aircraft grounded. PQ-12 lost the immunity given to PQ-10 and other winter convoys. Worse, while the ice pack was receding, it was receding more slowly than the days were lengthening. In the summer, waters north of Bear Island were ice free and in March and April, the ice pack kept convoys well south of that, much closer to the Luftwaffe's Lapland and Finnmark airfields.

The convoy had another worry. Luftwaffe and Kriegsmarine reinforcements were moving into Norway, and Germany was taking a greater interest in stopping the Arctic convoys. It had largely ignored them in 1941 due to the belief that the Soviet Union would soon surrender, but, with the first two months of 1942, it was clear it would take a major effort to defeat the Soviets. Part of that effort included cutting supplies heading to Russia, and the forces to do this were now available. Reinforcements sent to Norway to deter a British invasion could stay busy attacking convoys.

The battleship *Tirpitz* was there in January, and it was joined by most of the Kriegsmarine's surface units over the next two months. To reinforce Norway, the Kriegsmarine withdrew battlecruisers *Sharnhorst* and *Gneisenau*, and heavy cruiser *Prinz Eugen*, from Brest to Germany in a daring dash through the English Channel in February. The same month heavy cruisers *Admiral Scheer*, *Prinz Eugen* and five destroyers joined *Tirpitz*. March saw the arrival of heavy cruiser *Admiral Hipper* and six more destroyers. These ships operated out of Trondheim and Narvik.

To make the situation more critical for the convoys, long-range Fw 200 Condors moved to Trondheim-Vaernes in March. They had been sweeping the Atlantic Western Approaches to Great Britain, but as weather and visibility improved in the Arctic, attention was turned towards the Arctic convoys.

PQ-12 departed Reykjavík on 1 March 1942, and consisted of 18 transports. On the same day QP-8, with 15 merchant ships departed Murmansk. The initial escort for both convoys was small: four trawlers accompanied PQ-12 out of port, and provided coverage through 4 March. Similarly, QP-8's close escort was two minesweepers and two corvettes for U-boat protection augmented by two additional minesweepers which accompanied out of port were replaced by two Russian destroyers during the daylight hours of the first day. Three Royal Navy cruisers provided distant cover during its initial travels.

PQ-12's close escort swelled considerably on 4 March, when five antisubmarine whalers appeared. Two days later the light cruiser *Kenya* and two destroyers joined the close escort. Also at sea, providing distant cover was the Home Fleet, including battleship *Duke of York*, fleet carrier *Victorious*, heavy cruiser *Berwick* and six destroyers. It was there to guard against *Tirpitz*, reported at sea by British intelligence.

Tirpitz, along with four destroyers, was indeed at sea, having sailed at 1800 on 6 March. Luftwaffe scouts spotted PQ-12 at noon on 5 March. Unaware of *Victorious*, the German Admiral commanding, Otto Ciliax, hoped to catch PQ-12 or QP-8 somewhere south of the ice line between Jan Mayen and Bear Islands.

It proved an exercise in frustration. Lacking aerial reconnaissance, Ciliax managed to pass between the two convoys a few hours after they crossed paths at noon on 7 March.

Long-range Fw 200s arrived at Trondheim-Vaernes in March 1942, taking advantage of the improving spring weather in Arctic regions. Early detection also increased Arctic convoys' difficulties. (AC)

He ended up east of westbound QP-8 and west of eastbound PQ-12, passing within a few miles of QP-8 without sighting it. He detached his destroyers, which conducted a fruitless sweep for the convoys, and he then swept east. The only thing found was the straggling Russian freighter *Ijora*, laden with timber. It had fallen behind QP-8 and was promptly sunk by a German destroyer. The rest of QP-8 made it safely home.

PQ-12 turned north to avoid *Tirpitz*, reaching the ice line, and used a floatplane from *Kenya* to find a route east free of German warships. Some of its ships suffered ice damage from free-floating ice, and the convoy straggled but, regardless, all ships made it to Murmansk safely by 12 March.

After futilely seeking PQ-12 for another day, *Tirpitz* finally headed to port, its destroyers having departed earlier. At 0800 on 9 March, *Tirpitz* was discovered by one of six Albacores launched by *Victorious* while headed south towards Trondheim. Ciliax realized the single-engine aircraft was from an aircraft carrier; his first indication an aircraft carrier was around. He then sped towards Vestfjord and safety, while also calling for air cover. Before he reached Vestfjord the shadowing Albacores drew 12 torpedo-armed Albacores to *Tirpitz*, and all 12 dropped torpedoes. All 12 missed, the nearest passing 30ft astern of the battleship.

While the attack was unsuccessful, it increased the Kriegsmarine's fears of air attacks. The Kriegsmarine lacked aircraft carriers and depended on the Luftwaffe for air cover which arrived in the form a single He 115, 20 minutes after the attack. Three Ju 88s found the British task force that afternoon, and attacked, but it was too little, too late. They missed. After this, at Raeder's urging, Hitler ordered the Luftwaffe to protect Kriegsmarine operations.

By March, one Gruppe of Kampfgeschwader 30, I./KG30, was operating out of Banak and Bardafoss supporting operations in the Kola Peninsula. I./KG26 was also stationed at Banak, with 12 of its He 111 in the process of converting to carrying torpedoes. There were also 14 He 115 floatplanes in Finnmark capable of dropping torpedoes, and, later in March, III./KG30 was moved to Trondheim with II./KG30 joining it in April. Göring, entering into the spirit of the hunt, ordered Luftflotte 5 (which covered Norway) and all of its attached air units to conduct operations against Russian convoys. This included renewed attacks on ships which had already made Murmansk. Five-year old *Lancaster Castle*, 5,172grt, became the first casualty of Luftwaffe attention when it was dive-bombed in Murmansk roads and damaged on 24 March. It was attacked again on 14 April. This time dive bombers made five direct hits, sinking the ship.

The German battleship *Tirpitz* hunted Convoys PQ-12 and QP-8 when they sailed in March 1942. *Tirpitz* managed to miss both, sailing between them, and was chased back to port by Albacore torpedo bombers. (USNHHC)

The Fairey Albacore was intended as the Swordfish's replacement. In March 1942 Albacores from *Victorious* unsuccessfully attacked *Tirpitz*. While unsuccessful, the attack increased German reluctance to use *Tirpitz* at sea due to British carrier power. (SDA&SM)

The Luftwaffe's arrival as an active participant raised the stakes considerably, something the Allies failed to fully appreciate, instead continuing to focus on German surface units. The next set of convoys, PQ-13 and QP-9 respectively, sailed from Reykjavík on 20 March and Murmansk on 21 March. PQ-13 had 19 merchantmen with over 100,000 tons of cargo and three armed whalers to be transferred to the Soviet Union. QP-9 consisted of 18 ships with 80,000grt capacity.

The escort was heavy. Close escort for PQ-13 was light cruiser *Edinburgh*, three destroyers and two trawlers. A fleet oiler and escorting destroyer also accompanied the convoy on its opening leg to refuel the escorts before returning to Iceland. Close escort for QP-9 consisted of the cruiser *Trinidad*, a destroyer and two minesweepers. Five minesweepers, two Soviet and one Royal Navy destroyers accompanied QP-9 during its first two days. Cruiser *Kenya* was to have joined the convoy, leaving Kola on 22 March, but failed to find them. Covering both convoys was a large Home Fleet task force: battleships *King George V* and *Duke of York*, battlecruiser *Renown*, aircraft carrier *Victorious*, cruisers *Edinburgh* and *Kent*, and 11 destroyers.

Against them the Germans had two lines of U-boats seeking both convoys. Additionally, with days now longer than nights, the Luftwaffe had reconnaissance aircraft – Fw 200s, BV 138s, He 115s and Ju 88s – searching the waters between the Scandinavian coast and the ice line.

QP-9 made first contact with the enemy. On 23 March it was hit by an equinoctial gale, including heavy snowstorms, but the storm abated in the evening of 24 March without scattering the convoy. As the weather cleared a U-boat was spotted on the surface. Its lookouts were insufficiently alert. An escorting minesweeper, HMS *Sharpshooter*, rammed and sank *U-655*, before the U-boat could send a contact report. The damaged *Sharpshooter* detached from the convoy, proceeding independently to Leith for repairs. It was the last enemy contact QP-9 made, and the convoy proceeded to safety without being further molested.

PQ-13 was less fortunate. It missed the storm that battered QP-9, and was re-routed due east, avoiding one U-boat patrol line. (Information on the patrol line's location came from decryption of German signals.) This brought it closer to Luftwaffe airbases at Bardufoss and Banak than originally planned. The oiler and destroyer detached to refuel the Home Fleet destroyers shadowing PQ-13 and not until noon on 24 March did PQ-13 resume its north-northeasterly course, heading for a point south of Bear Island.

That evening a fresh storm hit PQ-13. By noon on 25 March it became so fierce it scattered the convoy. One whaler, HMS *Sulla*, disappeared during the storm, most probably capsizing from ice build-up. By dawn on 27 March the convoy was widely scattered and the weather, combined with the convoy's eastern progress, led the Home Fleet to return to port.

By 28 March, PQ-13 had dissolved into three clumps of ships, one with six merchant vessels and a whaler, a second with four merchant ships and the minesweepers, and a third where the escort warships had clustered. The rest, including the convoy commodore's ship *River Afton*, steamed independently towards Murmansk.

The Germans sent both aircraft and three large destroyers to hunt down the scattered convoy. Over the next two days Luftwaffe dive bombers sank two cargo ships and destroyers another one. The destroyers encountered *Trinidad* with destroyers *Fury* and *Eclipse*. In the battle that followed *Trinidad* crippled *Z26* before accidentally torpedoing itself. It was rescued by a mixed force of Soviet and British destroyers which sank *Z26*, and sent the other two German destroyers running to Kirkenes. On the 30th, as PQ-13's survivors straggled into Kola Inlet, two other ships were sunk by U-boats. One more ship, *Empire Starlight*, was bombed and sunk in harbour on 3 April.

These were horrific losses by the standards of previous Arctic convoys. Over 28,000 tons of shipping was lost, but three-quarters of the cargo arrived safely, so losses were considered acceptable. The Germans were launching a new offensive in Russia, so judged against the losses the Soviets were taking fighting the Germans, PQ-13's losses seemed trivial, especially to Stalin, who was demanding more deliveries from his Western allies.

Given Russia's peril, it was hard to refuse its demand by cutting back future convoys. Besides, PQ-13 and QP-9 destroyed two U-boats, one German destroyer and several Luftwaffe aircraft. The Admiralty dismissed the losses as having been due primarily to straggling and planned another round of Arctic convoys: PQ-14 to Russia and QP-10 homebound.

The escort again focused on protecting the convoy from Kriegsmarine surface ships. Over 40 Royal Navy warships were assigned to protect the 41 merchant ships of both convoys. This included a distant cover force with two fast battleships, an aircraft carrier, a heavy cruiser and eight destroyers. They were to stay west of 10 degrees East longitude, and intended to protect the convoy from an attempt by Kriegsmarine heavy units. By April, that included *Tirpitz*, *Scharnhorst*, *Admiral Scheer* and *Admiral Hipper* but, unknown to the British, fuel oil shortages were keeping these ships in port. The heavy cruiser *Norfolk* would patrol southwest

Storms were common on the Arctic run. QP-9 was battered by an equinoctial gale as it left Russia, and QP-13 hit a storm near Bear Island that was so fierce it scattered the convoy and sank a whaler. (AC)

The first ship sunk by aircraft while sailing in an Arctic convoy was the almost-new *Empire Cowper*, hit and sunk by a dive-bombing Ju 88 while sailing in QP-10. (AC)

of Bear Island, providing extra support to the two convoys as they passed through the area.

Providing close escort for PQ-14 was an initial escort of two minesweepers and four trawlers. These were joined south-southwest of Jan Mayen Island by a force consisting of *Edinburgh*, six destroyers, four corvettes and two trawlers. QP-10 was accompanied by light cruiser *Liverpool*, five destroyers, a minesweeper and two trawlers. They were accompanied by the usual assortment of minesweepers and Soviet destroyers the first day out of port.

PQ-14 was the biggest outbound convoy yet, its ships totalling nearly 150,000grt of capacity. It included heavy lift ship *Empire Bard*, which was to remain at Murmansk to facilitate unloading, the fleet oiler *Alderdale* and three tankers. There were six other British-flag cargo ships and 11 US-flag cargo ships in the convoy. The returning ships in QP-10 were made up of ships from PQ-12, along with a pair of quickly unloaded ships from PQ-13. They were in ballast or carried Russian timber.

PQ-14 left Reykjavík on 8 April; QP-10 left Murmansk two days later, on 10 April. PQ-14 ran into fog two nights out, and the worse ice yet encountered; growlers (small icebergs) broken off from the polar ice cap in the early spring weather. The dense fog scattered the convoy and growlers damaged two trawlers and several other ships. Nine returned to Iceland with the trawlers, too ice-battered to push on, and on 11 April only seven vessels, including the ice-damaged 12,000-ton tanker *Hopemount*, arrived at the rendezvous with their through escort. Six other ships continued independently until they encountered QP-10. All six joined QP-10, returning laden to Iceland rather than continuing to Murmansk alone.

While PQ-14 struggled with ice, QP-10 was fighting off the Luftwaffe. From 11 to 14 April the convoy beat off attacks by U-boats and Luftwaffe aircraft. *Empire Cowper*, new and 7,164grt went first, sunk by a KG 30 Ju 88 on 11 April, and a U-boat sank two freighters the next day. On 13 April aircraft crippled 5,486grt *Harpalion*, forcing the escort to sink it, but fog and a gale hid the convoy until 14 April, enabling it to escape three German destroyers seeking it, which were turned back by the weather.

Late on 14 April a Luftwaffe scout again found QP-10. The convoy was unmolested the next day and the days following because early on 15 April a BV-138 spotted PQ-14, shadowing the convoy until relieved by an Fw-200, and the Luftwaffe switched its attention to the laden inbound convoy. QP-10 proceeded home without further incident, gathering PQ-14's strays as it steamed west.

Meanwhile, the Luftwaffe and Kriegsmarine concentrated on PQ-14. Ju 88s began attacking on the afternoon of 15 April, continuing until nightfall. That day's attacks left the gunners of the convoy's cargo ships and warship escorts unimpressed. The next day KG 30 Ju 88s made continuous dive and level bombing attacks all day, coordinated with a U-boat wolf pack, but the Ju 88s were surprisingly ineffective, despite pressing their attacks, and they failed to score a single hit. However, a U-boat hit the convoy commodore's ship, *Empire Howard*, with three torpedoes. One exploded ammunition carried aboard the ship, splitting the vessel in two.

Early on 18 April the weather cleared and three German destroyers found PQ-14. They decided against tangling with it due to its strong escort, which included a cruiser and fog shielded the convoy for the rest of the day. Those aboard its ships could hear Luftwaffe aircraft low overhead.

Late the same day the escort was strengthened when four minesweepers and two Soviet destroyers joined the convoy. It sailed into Murmansk on 19 April. The convoy battles cost the Luftwaffe eight bombers, six shot down by ships in QP-10 and two by those in PQ-14, with another one damaged. It had cost the Allies five merchantmen of 31,000grt – an unfavourable exchange rate for the Allies.

The torpedo bomber appears: 21 April–15 June 1942

While the Luftwaffe had accounted for only three ships in PQ-14/QP-10, losses had mounted dramatically. Home Fleet leaders, responsible for protecting the Arctic convoys, were alarmed. Days were much longer than nights, allowing improved aerial reconnaissance, and the Admiralty advocated stopping the convoys during the summer months. Their concerns centred more on the threat posed by U-boats and *Tirpitz* than that of the Luftwaffe, however.

Pausing convoys was impossible politically, especially after only seven of 24 ships bound for Russia in PQ-14 arrived, with 16 having turned back. To stem the Axis's 1942 offensive the Soviets needed every aircraft, armoured vehicle and truck Britain and the US could send. With Stalin again threatening to make a separate peace if promised cargoes did not arrive, a shortfall in deliveries to Russia would have to be made up by larger convoys in the late spring and summer.

Meanwhile, as the weather improved Luftwaffe lethality approached critical mass. The two reinforcing Gruppes of KG 30 were in place and settled in, and the Luftwaffe was becoming more aggressive, with Ju 88s being used as bombers as well as for reconnaissance. Additionally, Ju 88s were augmenting the single flexible forward-firing machine gun by adding two fixed forward firing guns operated by the pilot. While only rifle-calibre guns, they significantly improved these bombers' ability to suppress antiaircraft fire from target ships, especially merchant vessels with a light antiaircraft battery.

Much of the Luftwaffe's ineffectiveness during PQ-13/QP-9 and PQ-14/QP-10 was due to a combination of inexperience and nervous excitement. Having grown used to Arctic conditions and gaining experience actually attacking shipping at sea meant pilots were more capable. However, another element contributed towards improving German effectiveness, the introduction of the aerial torpedo.

The most remarkable thing about the German aerial torpedo was the late date of its arrival. Every other major nation's air force, including Italy's *Regia Aeronautica* had had aerial torpedoes for years. Germany had no operational airborne torpedoes when World War II began, and would not until into the third year of the war.

Torpedoes were a naval weapon, the development of which fell to the Kriegsmarine. All maritime aircraft, even floatplanes flown off Kriegsmarine warships, belonged to the Luftwaffe, so the Kriegsmarine lacked incentive to divert its limited pre-war torpedo development funds away from U-boat and warship torpedoes. Instead, they chose to slow-walk aerial torpedo development. Even the outbreak of World War II did not change things since the Kriegsmarine continued ignoring aerial torpedoes.

Stalin was deaf to the Western Allies' complaints about losses on the Arctic run. Soviet soldiers like these were taking casualties in the tens of thousands each month fighting the Axis and Stalin felt the casualty totals among Allied sailors and mariners were too low to worry over. (AC)

An innovation introduced in PQ-15 was the inclusion of an antiaircraft ship. Auxiliary cruiser HMS *Ulster Queen* was an Irish Sea ferry converted to a warship by adding a battery of antiaircraft guns. It participated in Arctic convoys through the rest of 1942. (AC)

For the war's first year the Luftwaffe had no active interest in using torpedoes, and it was not until 1941 that the Luftwaffe did start researching aerial torpedoes. Interservice rivalry caused the Kriegsmarine to resist Luftwaffe efforts, and they denied the Luftwaffe access to Kriegsmarine test data on aerial torpedoes and attempted to block production of Luftwaffe torpedoes. The Luftwaffe had established its own torpedo development centre and contracted with an Italian manufacturer for torpedoes.

Things boiled over in December 1941, with Hitler awarding the Luftwaffe control over aerial torpedoes. Although aerial torpedoes became operational with the Luftwaffe in late 1941, they were only beginning to see use in combat by April 1942. Converting aircraft to carry torpedoes and training crews to use them consumed time and torpedo-equipped He 111s were finally operating out of Bardufoss by 1 May.

Arctic convoys were experiencing difficulties beyond enemy attacks in 1942. Facilities at Murmansk could not handle the upsurge in cargo volume and, once unloaded, cargoes often sat on quays and wharves, preventing more cargo from being unloaded. The heavy lift ship *Empire Bard*, intended to ease the problem, was one of the ships returning to Reykjavík due to ice damage. Ships from PQ-13 were still being unloaded when PQ-14 arrived, so the new ships had to wait their turn, anchored in the Kola Inlet anchorage.

Murmansk was close to Luftwaffe fields in Finland and the Luftwaffe recognized the laden ships at anchor offered a second opportunity to destroy Russian-bound cargoes before delivery. Air raids by both Ju 87 and Ju 88 dive bombers became frequent. In addition to *Empire Starlight*, sunk 3 April, *New Westminster City* was badly damaged by Luftwaffe bombs in April as it unloaded cargo.

Regardless, the next convoy cycle began in late April. Convoy PQ-15 departed Oban, Scotland, on 10 April, for Reykjavík, where it prepared to sail to Russia, departing Reykjavík on 25 April. QP-11 left Murmansk three days later, on 28 April.

PQ-15 had 25 cargo ships, including two icebreakers on passage to Russia. For the first time over half were US-flag ships, an indication of the growing influence of the United States. Many of PQ-15's ships were some of the 16 PQ-14 ships which turned back, including *Empire Bard*. Also travelling with the convoy was Force Q: *Grey Ranger*, an RFA oiler and its escort, Hunt-class escort destroyer *Ledbury*.

To deal with the aerial threat posed by the Luftwaffe, an auxiliary antiaircraft cruiser formed part of the escort and one of the freighters was a CAM ship. The antiaircraft cruiser, HMS *Ulster Queen* was a former Irish Sea ferry carrying mail and passengers. It could only make 18 knots, but that was fast enough to keep up with a convoy and in 1941 it was purchased by the Royal Navy. Armour was added, and the ship armed with three twin 4in gun turrets, four twin 2-pdrs, ten single 20mm Oerlikons and an antiaircraft gun director system.

The CAM ship, *Empire Morn*, carried one Hurricane Mk I on a catapult. A second was stored in the hold for use on the return voyage, a spare in case the first was used on the outbound trip. The two ships were inadequate antiaircraft protection, but they were the best Britain could do in spring 1942. The rest of the close escort consisted of a submarine, *Sturgeon*, four minesweepers, four ASW trawlers and six destroyers (including one Norwegian destroyer). The submarine was a first, intended to ambush Kriegsmarine vessels attacking the convoy. On 30 April they were joined by heavy cruiser *London* and light cruiser *Nigeria*.

QP-11 was made up of 11 freighters, most in ballast, and half were returning from PQ-13. The rest were ships from PQ-12, PQ-14 and a lone Soviet-flag ship crossing west for the first time. Its close escort was made up of *Edinburgh*, six elderly destroyers, four corvettes and a trawler. In addition to its escort duties *Edinburgh* also carried five tons of Soviet bullion – partial payment for munitions purchased from the US. Two Soviet destroyers and four British minesweepers accompanied the convoy the first day out.

To counter the threat a possible sortie by *Tirpitz* posed, the Home Fleet again provided distant cover. This time in addition to *King George V* and *Victorious*, it also included the US Navy battleship *Washington*. A British light cruiser, two US heavy cruisers and ten destroyers (four of which were American) rounded out the force. The US ships were added to replace Home Fleet warships temporarily sent to the Mediterranean to help with the relief of British-held Malta, then under siege by the Axis.

Hurricats in action

Catapult Armed Merchantmen (CAM) ships were ordinary merchant ships with an aircraft catapult mounted on their forecastle. They could launch a Hawker Hurricane fighter to engage attacking German aircraft, but recovering a launched aircraft at sea was impossible. The pilot had to find a friendly airbase within range, bail out of the aircraft or ditch at sea. Due to the catapult launch, these Hurricanes were known as 'Hurricats.'

CAM ships carried Sea Hurricanes, slightly modified Hurricane Mk IAs, and most were battle-weary Battle of Britain veterans, provided by the Royal Air Force. The pilots were also RAF members who belonged to Merchant Ship Fighter Unit (MSFU), but they signed ship's articles as if they were a civilian sailor when they and their aircraft were assigned to a ship.

There was only one CAM ship per convoy and they carried no reloads. Instead, an extra Hurricat was carried in the hold, for the return trip, but the ship needed to be in port to bring the spare out and install it on the catapult. Convoy commodores were reluctant to use CAM aircraft as it could potentially be more badly needed later. Compounding the reluctance was the relative ineffectiveness of the Hurricats. Hurricanes assigned to CAM duties were worn-out older aircraft, degrading their performance, and were armed with eight 0.303 machine guns rather than the more effective four 20mm cannon of later Hurricanes, which made it difficult to actually shoot down an enemy bomber. During the programme's existence, there were only nine combat launches of Hurricats. Four of which were on Arctic convoys which managed to shoot down five Luftwaffe bombers and chase off two reconnaissance aircraft.

The first Arctic use of Hurricats occurred on 26 April 1942, during Convoy QP-12. Having escaped detection until then, in late morning QP-12 was discovered by a searching BV 138 and Fw 200, which drew two Ju 88s to the convoy. *Empire Morn*, the convoy's CAM ship, launched its Hurricat, flown by Flying Officer John B. Kendal, and though his radio transmitter failed soon after launch, his receiver functioned.

He quickly drove off the BV 138 sending it into clouds and departing for home. Next, Kendal went after one of the two Ju 88s and after doggedly pursuing it he managed to knock out one engine. The Junkers jettisoned its bombs, and attempted to escape, but instead crashed within sight of the convoy. The other Ju 88 and Fw-200 broke off, leaving the convoy unmolested.

By then Kendal was low on fuel and headed for a destroyer near the convoy's stern. As he neared it, his engine cut out and the airplane dropped out of overcast into the sea. A second later Kendal appeared, parachute unopened – he did not open the canopy until he was 50ft above the water. The destroyer *Badworth* recovered Kendal but he was badly injured and died ten minutes after being brought aboard.

Despite his death, the flight was a success. It caused the Luftwaffe to lose contact with the convoy, allowing it to reach port safely with no further incident. This plate shows Kendal as he shoots down the Ju 88, his moment of triumph.

German destroyers were hunting HMS *Edinburgh*, a Town-class cruiser crippled by U-boat torpedoes while accompanying QP-11. *Edinburgh* was returning to Murmansk when the Germans caught it and, in the ensuing battle, a German destroyer was sunk, and *Edinburgh* again torpedoed. (AC)

The Allies were right to be concerned. The Luftwaffe and Kriegsmarine planned a major effort against these convoys. *Tirpitz* and the other Kriegsmarine surface units remained in port due to fuel oil shortages, but the Germans threw U-boats, destroyers and aircraft against the two convoys. This included, for the first time, torpedo bombers.

German reconnaissance aircraft found QP-11 on 29 April, one day out of Murmansk. Soviet air cover disappeared prematurely, allowing the convoy to be shadowed, and a Fw 200 Condor spotted PQ-14 250 miles southwest of Bear Island near midnight on 30 April. The Germans had two targets, but QP-11 was closer and initial attacks focused on it.

Near dawn on 30 April, 'Huff-Duff' radio direction finders detected homing signals near QP-11 from *U-88*. Escorts forced *U-88* under, but at least three other U-boats were stalking the convoy. Two U-boats caught *Edinburgh* alone, at night stations ahead of the convoy, and although four torpedoes from *U-436* missed, two from *U-456* hit, blowing off *Edinburgh*'s stern and its two inboard propellers, and flooding one boiler room.

Edinburgh turned back to Murmansk at two knots, the fastest speed it was capable of making on two propellers. Two British destroyers were detached to accompany it, as were the two Russian destroyers that were returning to Murmansk anyway. The Germans, eager to finish off the crippled cruiser, dispatched three large Narvik-class destroyers to hunt it down.

QP-11 continued on. Dawn of 1 May found it steaming parallel to the edge of the ice and 150 miles east of Bear Island. In the morning twilight six Ju 88s attacked. The bombs, dropped prematurely, missed, and U-boats made runs at the convoy the rest of the morning. At 1400, the convoy encountered the three German destroyers hunting *Edinburgh*.

A four-hour battle ensued in which a spirited defence by PQ-11's escort kept the German destroyers at bay. The destroyer *Amazon* was hit twice in the battle, but not sunk, and the convoy's only other casualty was the 2847grt Soviet freighter *Tsiolkovski*, sunk after it straggled and was torpedoed. The Germans retired seeking their primary target, *Edinburgh*. On 1 May, QP-11 was joined by Force Q which refuelled the escort. Thereafter, QP-11 continued to port unmolested.

The Germans found *Edinburgh* on 2 May, 250 miles east of where it left QP-11. It was only accompanied by the two British destroyers and four minesweepers (the Russian destroyers had returned to port, low on fuel). One German destroyer, *Hermann Schoemann*, attacked alone, and was crippled by *Edinburgh*. The other two destroyers then appeared, crippling both British destroyers and torpedoing *Edinburgh*. The German ships withdrew, recovering the crew from the sinking *Hermann Schoemann* before returning to port. *Edinburgh* was similarly abandoned, its crew taken aboard the minesweepers before a British destroyer torpedoed it.

Meanwhile it was PQ-15's turn to be attacked. At 2200hrs on 1 May, six Ju 88s appeared. One attacked *London* and was shot down short of the cruiser, splashing ahead of *Nigeria*, which ran over it. The rest attacked the trawlers, but all bombs dropped missed, largely due to the vigorous antiaircraft fire thrown up by the escorts.

That same day, after the distant escort ran into fog, destroyer *Punjabi* turned in front of *King George V*. The battleship ran over *Punjabi*, cutting it in two. Its stern sank immediately and the depth charges exploded, further damaging the battleship. Then, on 2 May, PQ-15's escorts found, attacked and sank a submarine. It proved to be the Polish *Jastrząb*, part of the submarine picket line watching for Kriegsmarine warships. It was 100nmi off station when PQ-15 encountered it. Fortunately, its crew was recovered before it sank.

The next day, 3 May, opened equally badly. In pre-dawn twilight six KG 26 He 111s swept in at wave-top height on a torpedo run. They were undetected until they dropped their torpedoes, though antiaircraft fire shot down two, and damaged a third so badly it crashed returning home. Yet torpedoes struck three freighters, *Cape Corso*, the convoy commodore's *Bovaton*, and Polish-flagged *Jutland*, totalling 15,800grt. All three sank, although 137 survivors were rescued. It was the first aerial torpedo attack against an Arctic convoy.

U-boats attempted to attack for the rest of the day, but were driven off by the escorts. At sunset twilight, KG 30 Ju 88s bombed the convoy. One bomb damaged the trawler *Cape Palliser* and one Ju 88 was shot down. The escort continued driving off U-boats through most of 4 May, until a gale blew up in the evening. Clouds then shrouded PQ-15 until it reached Murmansk on 5 May.

Soon after PQ-15 arrived *Trinidad* left Murmansk. Damaged during PQ-13 it had slowly been making temporary repairs at Murmansk to make it seaworthy enough to return to Britain. Its hull was patched up, but one boiler room was unusable, though it could make 20 knots, fast enough for the passage. *Trinidad* left Murmansk on 13 May, loaded with survivors from *Edinburgh*, *Jastrząb* and various sunken merchant ships. It was accompanied by four destroyers, of which two, *Forester* and *Foresight*, had been damaged during PQ-15 in the fight with the German destroyers. They had temporary repairs and were not fully effective.

Convoy PQ-16 engaged in a six-day running battle with Luftwaffe aircraft between 25 May and 31 May, undergoing attacks by Ju 88s and He 111s. Ju 88s managed to bomb and cripple the Hog Islander *Carlton*, which was towed back to Iceland. (AC)

First Blood for the Torpedo Corps

At 0130hrs on 3 May 1942, six Heinkel He 111 bombers of I. Gruppe,
Kampfgeschwader 26, the Luftwaffe's new torpedo bomber force, attacked
convoy PQ-15, making the first German torpedo bomber attack of World War
II. Three ships were hit, two sank and one was damaged, later sunk by *U-251*.

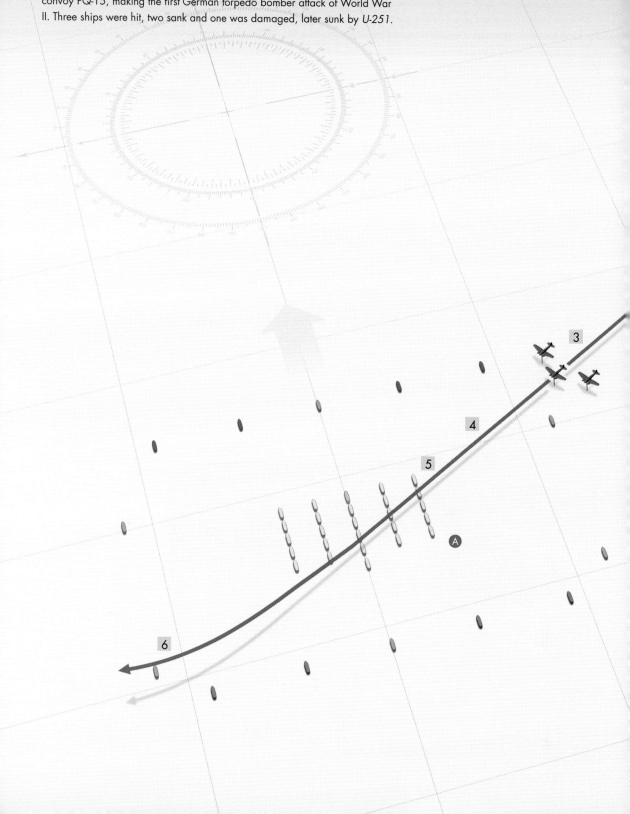

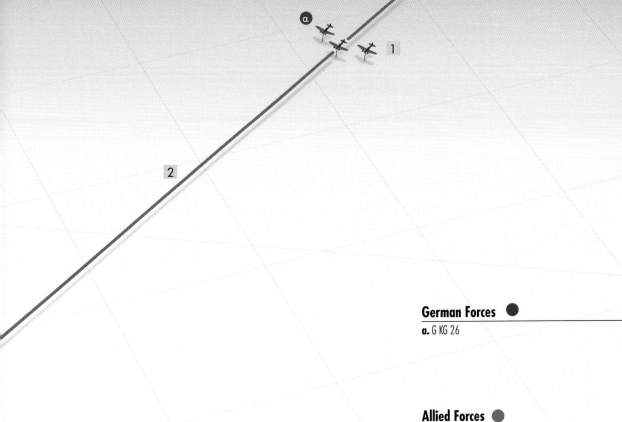

German Forces ●
a. G KG 26

Allied Forces ●
A Convoy PQ 15

EVENTS

1 0130hrs. Six He 111s appear on the horizon.

2 0133hrs. General quarters sounds in the convoy.

3 0135hrs. Antiaircraft fire begins, two He 111s are hit and shot down (a third is damaged severely enough to fail to make landfall).

4 0136hrs. Surviving He 111s drop their torpedoes.

5 0137hrs. Freighters *Botavon*, *Cape Corso* and *Jutland* hit by torpedoes. *Botavon* and *Cape Corso* sink (*Jutland* sunk later by *U-251*).

6 0139hrs. Surviving He 111s escape.

Things went wrong almost immediately. The promised air cover was almost non-existent, three Soviet Hurricanes instead of the expected six Hurricanes and 12 PE3 fighters. A German reconnaissance aircraft found *Trinidad* on 14 May and was joined by others, which shadowed the force. Meanwhile, KG 26 He 111s at Bardufoss and Ju 88s out of Banak were fuelling and arming up.

At 2100hrs *Trinidad*'s radar spotted incoming waves of aircraft to the south and south-southeast at 15, 30, 40 and 60 miles. The first attack came an hour later. Over 20 KG 30 Ju 88 dive bombers came out of the clouds pressing their dives nearly into the sea. Attacking destroyers and cruisers, they scored no hits. Meanwhile, the British put up an intense antiaircraft barrage, and 37 minutes later eight He 111 torpedo bombers arrived. Their first pass was disrupted by antiaircraft fire, but they made a second pass, dropping torpedoes.

Trinidad turned to evade three torpedoes coming towards it. While they were passing along either side of *Trinidad*, a lone Ju 88 dived out of the clouds and dropped four bombs. Three near-missed, ripping off temporary plating patching *Trinidad*'s port side, and driving splinters through the port and starboard hull plating near the bow. The fourth hit amidships, penetrating the Admiral's cabin and detonated in the mess decks, blowing another hole to starboard.

Although *Trinidad*'s antiaircraft battery shot down the attacking Ju 88, *Trinidad* was doomed. As fires raged, *Trinidad* was ordered abandoned. After taking off the surviving crew (63 aboard died), *Trinidad* was torpedoed by a British destroyer to scuttle it.

The next convoy cycle, involving PQ-16 and QP-12, was scheduled for late May. Both John Tovey, commanding the Home Fleet, and Dudley Pound, First Lord of the Admiralty, wanted to delay future convoys until after the autumnal equinox. Both men felt the perpetual daylight of the Arctic summer would leave convoys easy targets for aircraft, whose effectiveness had been starkly demonstrated over the past three months, but they were overridden by Churchill and Roosevelt. The campaign in Russia was reaching a climax and Stalin knew there were 90 ships with supplies for Russia in Iceland and the United States, and he demanded their content. In 1942 those supplies could not be provided across the Pacific or through the Persian Gulf and Churchill bowed to that pressure, ordering a yet bigger convoy to sail. PQ-16 left Reykjavík with 36 merchantmen on 21 May accompanied by a minesweeper and four trawlers. One of the freighters, *Empire Lawrence*, was a CAM ship.

Two days later, PQ-16 was joined by yet another auxiliary antiaircraft cruiser, *Alynbank*, converted in a manner similar to *Ulster Queen*. With it came three British and one Free French corvettes, and two submarines. Force Q, this time made up of RFA oiler *Black Ranger* with destroyer *Ledbury*, were present to refuel the escort of both convoys. The Kriegsmarine moved panzerschiffs *Sheer* and *Lutzow* to Narvik with an accompanying oiler. For protection against them four British cruisers and three destroyers were to accompany PQ-16 as far as Bear Island.

QP-12 departed the Kola Inlet on the same day PQ-16 set sail. It had 14 ships, most from QP-15, including CAM ship *Empire Morn*. For close escort it had *Ulster Queen*, five destroyers and four trawlers. Accompanying both to 30 degrees East were two Soviet destroyers and four minesweepers.

To guard against a sortie by *Tirpitz*, a Home Fleet force made up of *Duke of York*, *Washington*, *Victorious*, two heavy cruisers and 13 destroyers (four US and nine British) was formed. Additionally, the Soviets promised to attack Axis airfields in Finnmark and Lapland with 200 bombers to suppress the Luftwaffe. The promise was inadequately kept and only one raid with 20 bombers was sent.

As before, the westbound convoy was spotted first. A Condor sighted QP-12 on 25 May and was relieved in late morning by a BV 138 and two Ju 88s. *Empire Morn* launched its Hurricane, seeking the BV 138, but the Hurricane's pilot lost the BV 138 in the clouds and returned to the convoy. There he spotted a Ju 88, and attacked it. He shot it down, and the

On 3 May 1942 six He 111 torpedo bombers attacked PQ-15. For the loss of three He 111s they hit three ships, sinking *Cape Corso*, *Bovaton*, and *Jutland*, a favourable rate of exchange. (AC)

other Luftwaffe aircraft fled. Low on fuel he bailed out near a destroyer but unfortunately his parachute opened late, and he died from injuries after hitting the water. His sacrifice however was not in vain. He drove off the shadowing aircraft, delaying further detection and attack until after QP-12 crossed paths with PQ-16 three hours later.

Attention then switched to the now-closer PQ-16. Starting at 1910 on 25 May, PQ-16 fought a six-day running battle with the Luftwaffe and U-boats before it made port. The Luftwaffe had been trailing PQ-16 since 0600, but the first attack came at 1910, five hours after PQ-16 passed QP-12, when 19 torpedo-carrying He 111s attacked under clear skies.

Empire Lawrence launched its Hurricane, which set one He 111 afire and damaged a second before being shot down by 'friendly' antiaircraft fire. The pilot, although injured, was recovered by HMS *Volunteer*, a V-class destroyer. None of the torpedoes hit their targets.

Six Ju 88 dive bombers struck next, damaging 5,127grt *Carlton*; the Hog Islander having to be towed back to Iceland by a trawler. The day closed with a final attack by 12 Ju 88s, which scored no hits. In addition to shooting down the Hurricane, the convoy's guns downed two Luftwaffe aircraft that day.

Syros, 6,191grt, was torpedoed and sunk by *U-703* at 0305hrs on 26 May. That prompted the cruisers to detach well west of Bear Island and join QP-12. German surface ships were remaining in port, removing the main reason for the cruisers' presence, but their departure significantly weakened PQ-16's antiaircraft defences. Fortunately, although the Luftwaffe approached PQ-16 several times over the next 24 hours, with both He 111s and Ju 88s, none of the attacks were pressed home. The barrage from the remaining ships, especially *Alynbank*, discouraged anything beyond testing attacks.

Pack ice forced PQ-16 south on 27 May, bringing it closer to Luftwaffe airbases. Attacking through a broken cloud base at 3,000ft, Ju 88s and He 111 attacked in coordinated waves throughout the day. The convoy had early warning of all attacks thanks to a German-speaking RAF team aboard *Alynbank*, who monitored Luftwaffe radio communications.

That intelligence only alerted the convoy as to when and how many aircraft were attacking, but it ensured guns were manned, without increasing their numbers. Over the course of 27 May air attacks sank four transports, including *Empire Morn*, and damaged three others,

A rare attack by Ju 87 Stukas occurred on the final day of PQ-16. They attacked the Arkhangelsk contingent of the convoy as it followed the narrow channel cut through the ice to the harbour, but were driven off by antiaircraft fire. (AC)

including the convoy commodore's *Ocean Voice*, and Polish destroyer *Garland*. *Garland*, hit early in the day, had half its guns, and its antennae and director control knocked out, further reducing PQ-16's antiaircraft defences. By the end of the day, many ships were low on ammunition.

The Luftwaffe did not return the next day until 2130hrs, but by then PQ-16 had been reinforced by three Soviet destroyers with heavy antiaircraft batteries. Attacks continued through the early hours of 29 May, but none of the attacks on 28 or 29 May did damage.

On 29 May, PQ-16 was reinforced by six Murmansk-based minesweepers. It also split that day, 140nm from Kola Inlet. Six ships, accompanied by *Alynbank* and destroyer *Martin*, proceeded to Arkhangelsk. The rest, with a much-weakened antiaircraft capability continued to Murmansk. The two parts were attacked by Ju 88s at 2330hrs, while still in sight of each other, when 18 Ju 88s attacked the Murmansk-bound ships, and 15 hit the Arkhangelsk ships. The convoys suffered no damage, and two Ju 88s were downed.

Thereafter Soviet fighters, including Hurricanes delivered earlier, protected the Murmansk ships from further attack. The Arkhangelsk contingent however were attacked by Stukas while proceeding single-file through a narrow channel cut in the ice of the White Sea. *Alynbank* and *Martin* drove the Stukas off, although *Martin*'s magazines were so empty it ended up firing armour-piercing rounds at the aircraft.

The Luftwaffe ascendant: 16 June–20 July 1942

PQ-16 underscored the danger of Luftwaffe aircraft. In his after-action report on PQ-16 Commander Richard Onslow, who commanded the escort, recommended the use of more antiaircraft ships, the addition of dedicated rescue ships and fire-fighting tugs. (One freighter exploded after fires aboard it burned out of control, but it could have been saved by a fireboat.) Most importantly, he recommended inclusion of an escort carrier. The single Hurricane carried aboard *Empire Morn* successfully and single-handedly broke up the first aerial attack on PQ-16, and an escort carrier could ensure continuous fighter presence during the perpetual sunlight of the Arctic summer.

Again, the Admiralty and Tovey recommended the next convoy be postponed, but June was close to the Axis high-water mark during its 1942 Russian offensive and aircraft and tanks brought by the Arctic convoys were making a difference. Moreover, Arkhangelsk was open again, and with improved port facilities at Murmansk, Russia's ability to unload more cargo had risen.

The Germans planned to meet the next Arctic convoy with Operation *Rösselsprung*, a major effort by Kriegsmarine surface ships to intercept a convoy at sea. Detected by Allied intelligence, the threat so mesmerized the Admiralty that it led to disaster at the hands of U-boats and Luftwaffe aircraft. (USNHHC)

The Admirals' concern was fuelled by knowledge that the Kriegsmarine was planning a major surface operation to stop the next convoy. Allied codebreaking revealed the existence and outline of Operation *Rösselsprung* (a knight's move in chess). In it Raeder intended to deploy *Tirpitz, Hipper, Scheer* and *Lützow* in an operation against the next Arctic convoy.

When *Rösselsprung* eventually occurred, it collapsed under the weight of its own complexity and operational rules, but it had mesmerized British leadership. They became obsessed with the threat posed by German battleships and cruisers, and concentrated on that threat almost to the exclusion of all others. Admiral Tovey advocated having the convoy reverse course and steam west if news were received that *Tirpitz* and heavy cruisers were at sea before the convoy reached 10 degrees East (when it would be safer continuing east). Pound had another solution: disperse the convoy and scatter the ships if it came under attack by heavy units. Scattering involved sending the convoy's merchant ships on diverging courses 5–10 degrees apart.

Both solutions ignored the real threat, the Luftwaffe. Reversing course kept the ships within range of Luftwaffe attack much longer and scattering left the ships even more exposed. One thing diminishing PQ-16 losses was the convoy's tight formation. It made it more difficult for the Luftwaffe to attack by concentrating the convoy's antiaircraft coverage, and it also reduced exposure to U-boat attack because these had to attack submerged during daylight hours when escorts were present. Scattering the convoy allowed U-boats to make surface attacks on individual merchantmen, a return to the era of the deck gun.

By mid-June the Luftwaffe had 15 He 115 floatplanes, 30 Ju 87s, 42 He 111s and 103 Ju 88 bombers available in the far north. For scouting, they could call on 8 Fw 200s, 22 Ju 88s and 44 BV 138 reconnaissance aircraft. These could also attack under some circumstances and crews of torpedo-carrying aircraft had undergone further training to improve torpedo accuracy and effectiveness.

Despite the Luftwaffe's strength, it would not cooperate with *Rösselsprung* for fear of compromising its own offensive against the next convoys. As a result, Dönitz set up two lines of U-boats to scout for the convoy, three near the Denmark Strait (with orders to shadow the convoy rather than attack it), and eight more in a line near Jan Mayen.

The Independence Day attacks

On 4 July 1942 (US Independence Day – with the British warships guarding the convoy congratulating the US warships) the Luftwaffe launched three air attacks against PQ-17. Attacks began in the morning and continued through to 2123hrs. The Allies successfully drove off all three air attacks, showing the convoys' effectiveness against air attack.

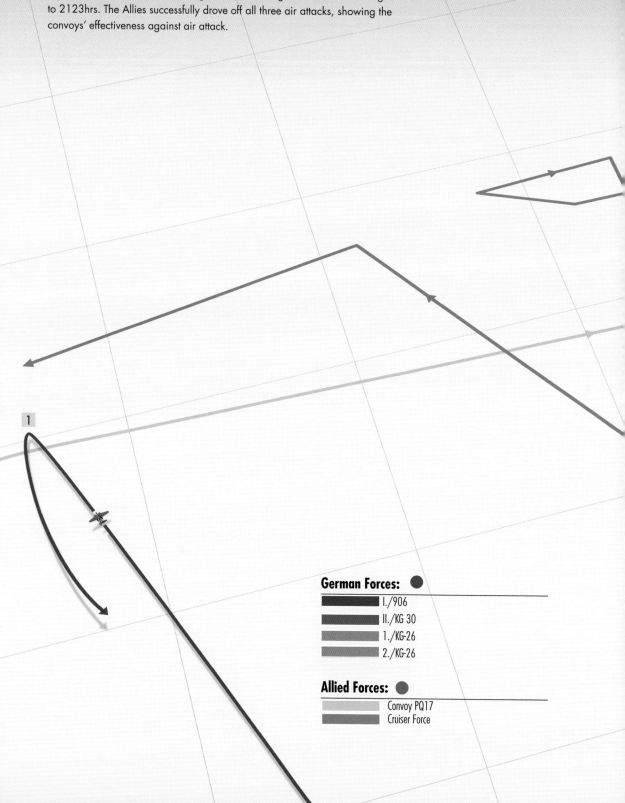

German Forces: ●

▬	I./906
▬	II./KG 30
▬	1./KG-26
▬	2./KG-26

Allied Forces: ●

▬	Convoy PQ17
▬	Cruiser Force

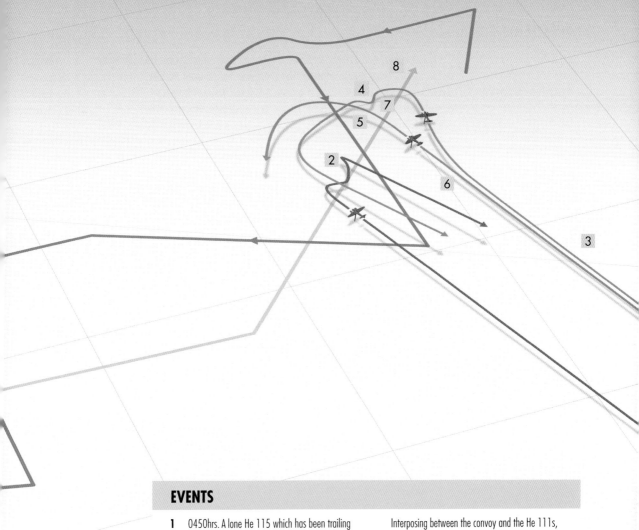

EVENTS

1   0450hrs. A lone He 115 which has been trailing PQ-17 cuts its engines, silently gliding into the convoy, where it drops a torpedo that narrowly misses two ships before hitting Liberty Ship *Christopher Newport*. The He 115 escapes, uninjured; *Christopher Newport* is scuttled due to its damage.

2   1930–2000hrs. Ju 88s make a series of half-hearted bombing attacks at 1,000ft. They fail to press home the attacks, deterred by heavy antiaircraft fire.

3   2015hrs. Two groups of He 111 torpedo bombers approach convoy PQ-17, guided in by a shadowing Ju 88 sent to bring the torpedo bombers to the convoy. They split up when the convoy is sighted.

4   2020hrs. One group of He 111s attacks the convoy from its port quarter.

5   2022–2024hrs. US destroyer *Wainwright* leaves the convoy at 32 knots to break up the port attack.

Interposing between the convoy and the He 111s, its antiaircraft fire causes this attack to be aborted. One He 111 is shot down, the rest drop their torpedoes before reaching *Wainwright*.

6   2020–2025hrs. The second group of He 111s attack the convoy's starboard quarter. The British escorts draw in to protect the convoy with close concentrated antiaircraft fire. This allows nine of these He 111s to reach torpedo range before being seriously engaged.

7   2027hrs. Three ships are hit by torpedoes: Russian tanker *Azerbaijan* is damaged, British freighter *Navarino* and US Liberty Ship *William Hooper* are sunk.

8   2215hrs. Despite successfully driving off all U-boat and aircraft attacks with a loss of only three ships, the Admiralty orders PQ-17 to scatter due to fear of a possible attack by the *Tirpitz*, whose location is unknown.

OPPOSITE PQ-17/QP-13

Furthermore, Germany had other intelligence on convoy movements. B-Dienst, Germany's signal intelligence service, broke Naval Cipher No 3, used for communications with convoy escorts, in February 1942. By March, B-Dienst was reading up to 80 percent of this traffic, deciphering it in near-real time. The Germans knew when a convoy was coming and where it would be going.

British planning for convoys PQ-17 and QP-13 was the most elaborate to that date. As usual the two convoys each had a close escort, with a covering force intended to protect the convoys against cruisers and destroyers, and a distant force to monitor *Tirpitz*. There was also a decoy convoy, a new innovation.

PQ-17 was made up of 41 merchant vessels, five of which were RFA: fleet oilers *Aldersdale* and *Grey Ranger*, and rescue ships *Rathlin*, *Zaafaran* and *Zamalek*. *Aldersdale*, with one destroyer, formed Force Q this time. *Grey Ranger* was supposed to go to Russia to provide reserve fuel for British warships there, though circumstances forced the two ships to swap roles. Rescue ships were being used for the first time on PQ-17, and one CAM ship, *Empire Tide*, was in the convoy. The ships carried 297 aircraft, 594 tanks and 4,246 military vehicles – half tracks, gun carriers and trucks – and 150,000 tons of cargo and military goods.

QP-13 had 35 ships, of which 15 were returning from PQ-16 and seven from PQ convoys which sailed earlier in 1942. The rest came from convoys which departed for Russia in 1941. Most ships were in ballast; five carried timber or lumber. There was no CAM ship, having been sunk in PQ-16.

Close escort for PQ-17 consisted of two auxiliary antiaircraft cruisers, HMS *Palomares* and *Pozarica*, eight destroyers, four corvettes, three minesweepers and four trawlers. The minesweepers and trawlers departed with the convoy; the rest joined at sea. The auxiliary antiaircraft cruisers were two fast fruit boats with eight 4in guns, advanced radar and an aircraft tracking station added.

QP-13's close escort was made up primarily of the close escort of PQ-16 and the destroyers sent to escort *Trinidad* on its final voyage. It had five destroyers, four corvettes, two minesweepers, two trawlers and a submarine. One destroyer was Polish; one corvette Free French. One British and three Soviet destroyers and four minesweepers accompanied the convoy on the first two days out of Murmansk.

The Luftwaffe increased its presence in the Arctic throughout June. When PQ-17 sailed, the Luftwaffe had 103 Ju 88 bombers, including torpedo-carrying Ju 88, and another 22 reconnaissance Ju 88s in Finnmark and Lapland bases. (AC)

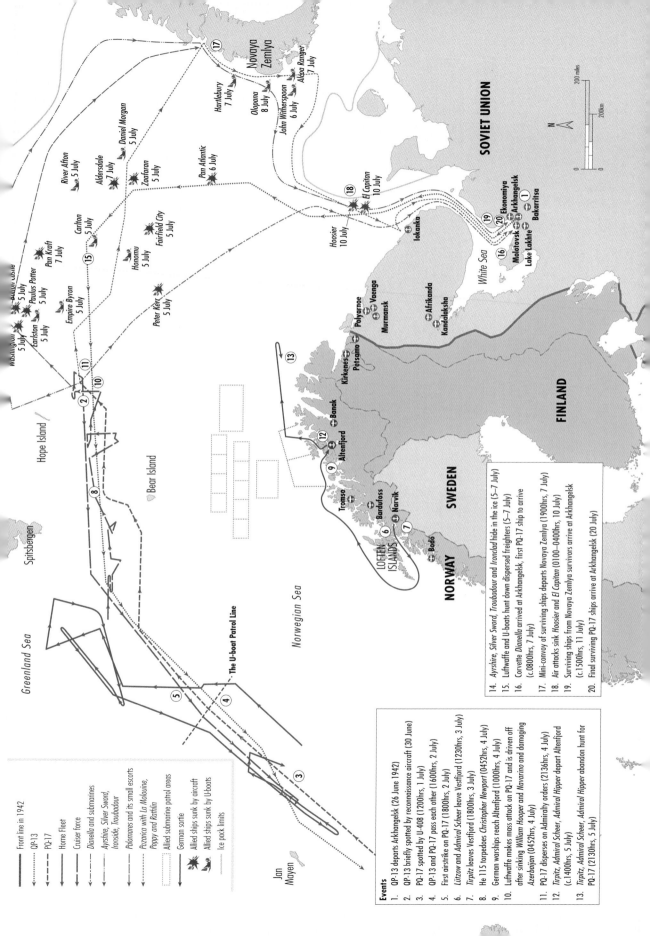

Convoy PQ-17 sailed for Russia from Iceland on 27 June 1942. It was the largest convoy yet, with 41 ships. It is shown here off Iceland's western coast shortly after departing Reykjavík. (USNHHC)

The covering force of cruisers consisted of two County-class Royal Navy heavy cruisers, two US Navy heavy cruisers and a destroyer each from the two nations. This Cruiser Force was supposed to cover the convoy as far east as Bear Island where, if necessary to protect it, they would shadow QP-13. If they received intelligence the German cruisers were after PQ-17, they could continue east, but no further than 25 degrees East. In the contingency the convoy was ordered scattered to protect it from Kriegsmarine heavy units, the destroyers of its close escort were to rendezvous with the Cruiser Force, to reinforce its attack on the German cruisers.

There was also the distant force, again intended to monitor *Tirpitz*. It again consisted of *Duke of York*, *Washington* and *Victorious*, this time with one British heavy cruiser and light cruiser, and 12 destroyers, two US and ten British. As before, these were to remain east of Bear Island.

Finally, to draw Kriegsmarine warships and U-boats away from PQ-17, the Royal Navy planned a distraction: a dummy convoy. To simulate a new raid on Norway, antiaircraft cruisers *Sirius* and *Curacoa* and five destroyers accompanied a 'convoy' made up of the First Minelaying Squadron and several colliers. These were to steam towards northern Norway, where Britain previously launched commando raids in hopes of drawing the Kriegsmarine and Luftwaffe into the Norwegian Sea and out of the Barents Sea where PQ-17 would pass.

QP-13 started the operation, departing Arkhangelsk on 26 June. At Kola Inlet, on 28 June, it picked up additional ships from Murmansk, and the convoy then sailed across the eastern Barents Sea with a perpetual escort of clouds and fog. Dead reckoning was required for navigation, but the thick weather concealed QP-13 from searchers. It was spotted briefly on 30 June, and quickly lost again, but was finally clearly detected on 2 July, the day it passed PQ-17. It picked up Force Q that day, which returned with it, and the Germans ignored it thereafter because PQ-17 was the more attractive target.

PQ-17 set out from Reykjavík on 27 June. Most of its ships were scheduled to arrive at Arkhangelsk and only eight were to detach to Murmansk. Problems piled up almost immediately. Liberty ship *Richard Bland* ran aground off Iceland and had to return, escorted by a trawler and a tug. The convoy took a northerly route, intending to pass north of Bear Island, but in the Denmark Strait it ran across drifting ice and two ships took ice damage, transport *Exford* and *Grey Ranger* – a growler opened *Grey Ranger*'s bow, and *Exford* returned to Reykjavík. *Grey Ranger* was too damaged to reach Russia, but too important to return to Reykjavík so replaced *Aldersdale* as the Force Q tanker, while *Aldersdale* was tasked to go to Russia.

The decoy convoy sailed from Scapa Flow on 29 June, attempting to convince the Germans an assault on Norway was imminent. Unfortunately, Luftwaffe reconnaissance aircraft were scouring waters north of the bait convoy and never spotted it. It returned to Scapa Flow to depart once more on 1 July; by then PQ-17 was passing Jan Mayen Island. The Cruiser Force left Seidesfiord at 0200 the same day, steaming at 20 knots to their covering position, but again the Germans missed the decoy. Instead, at 1400 a Fw 200 spotted PQ-17 fifty miles east of Jan Mayen.

Captain Jack Broome, commanding the escort, employed a new escort technique. He stationed most escorts in a ring 3,000yds from the convoy's merchant ships for antisubmarine protection and, when an air raid was expected, the escorts drew in to 1,000yds. The two antiaircraft ships were just within the outer columns of the merchant ships.

Additionally, the rescue ships had radio direction finders. This allowed them to work with the destroyers to fix positions of shadowing U-boats which could be attacked to keep them from transmitting the convoy's position. This maximized antiaircraft fire when needed, while permitting early U-boat protection. They would soon need both kinds of protection, as for the next four days they would be under almost continuous attack.

PQ-17 had been spotted by *U-408* at noon, even before it caught the Condor on radar. It would also be detected by *U-255* at 1530hrs. Neither boat attacked or even trailed the convoy, but they did radio reports. Dönitz had a patrol line set up east of these boats, halfway between Jan Mayen and Bear Islands, but the Luftwaffe and Kriegsmarine were largely operating independently and shared information reluctantly.

Regardless, PQ-17 had a continuous escort of German aircraft after the initial contact. A BV 137 relieved the Condor soon after it arrived and followed the convoy. The Cruiser Force sent a Walrus floatplane to cover the convoy, but the aircraft avoided tangling with the shadowing Germans.

At 1800hrs on 2 July, the first airstrike was launched against PQ-17. It was made as the Cruiser Force rendezvoused with PQ-17. Seven to nine He 115 launched torpedoes at

A BV 138 spotted Convoy PQ-17 on 1 July, a few hours after the convoy moved east of Jan Mayen Island. This photograph was taken from the aircraft, providing the first solid information about its position and size. (USNHHC)

He 115s made two torpedo attacks on PQ-17. The first, by seven aircraft on 2 July was unsuccessful. The second, by a lone He 115, succeeded in hitting *Christopher Newport*, which was subsequently scuttled. (AC)

Pozarica, but missed. They broke off when the antiaircraft ship and the approaching US destroyer *Rowan* began firing. No hits were scored, and one He 115 was shot down. Its crew was recovered by another He 115, which then flew off.

The Cruiser Force cruisers moved independently, staying north of PQ-17, and covering the convoy with occasional Walrus overflights. Meanwhile, at 2000hrs on 2 July, *Tirpitz* with four destroyers left Trondheim for Vestfiord. *Lutzow* and *Scheer* left Vestfiord at 1230hrs the following day but *Lützow* and three destroyers then ran aground and had to return. *Tirpitz* sailed at 1830hrs, and both groups hugged the Norwegian coast, putting in at Altenfjord at 1000hrs on 4 July. Their orders would not let them enter the Barents Sea until they confirmed no British carriers were operating there.

Meanwhile, PQ-17 continued east. Luftwaffe aircraft discovered the presence of the cruisers but fog shrouded the convoy through 3 July. Early on 4 July it lifted, forming a low cloud cover over PQ-17. The convoy was 60 miles north of Bear Island when an He 115 came out of the clouds and, despite antiaircraft fire, dropped a torpedo. At 0452hrs the torpedo struck Liberty ship *Christopher Newport* in the engine room. Unable to proceed, Broome ordered *Newport* scuttled, rather than risk towing it to safety. The Luftwaffe had its first kill.

BV 138s re-established contact with PQ-17 in mid-morning. As the forenoon watch began, every US ship in the convoy lowered its flag, replacing it with new, larger colours in celebration of US Independence Day (as did the US warships in the Cruiser Force). At noon, Admiral Hamilton received permission to pass 25 degrees East and continue covering PQ-17, but Tovey limited that permission, refusing to allow it unless Hamilton got definite word *Tirpitz* was in port. Hamilton then moved south of the convoy for extra protection.

Throughout the afternoon of 4 July, PQ-17 was subject to half-hearted harassing attacks by Ju 88s, BV-138s and He 115s. These were driven off by antiaircraft fire, including that of the Cruiser Force. One U-boat made a submerged attack which missed, and the only air attack which caused issues was one on *Wainwright*, a US destroyer. The Cruiser Force destroyers had been refuelling one by one from *Aldersdale* and when *Wainwright*'s turn came, it was near-missed by a bomber.

At 2025hrs the Luftwaffe made its first mass attack on PQ-17. A mixed force of 25 torpedo-bearing He 111s and Ju 88s attacked the escorts. The long-range antiaircraft fire of the US destroyers, especially *Wainwright*, broke up the attack. One He 111 was shot down, and the rest of the first wave failed to press home its attack.

The second wave was pressed home, however. They came in so low and close that several ships were damaged by over-eager antiaircraft gunners. One torpedo blew the bottom out of Liberty Ship *William Hooper*; a second sank British freighter *Navarino*. A Soviet tanker, *Azerbaijan*, was hit, but was able to continue at nine knots. Three He 111s were shot down, including both of those sinking ships. The cruisers joined the battle with antiaircraft fire, and the Luftwaffe broke off the fight.

Morale was high. PQ-17 had driven off an air attack and demonstrated an ability to defend against these attacks, and although there were seven U-boats in the area, they were reluctant to attack the heavily defended convoy in daylight. Bear Island was 160 miles behind them and *Empire Tide* was ready to launch its Hurricane to drive off the remaining BV 138 shadowing the convoy. Then disaster struck.

At 2111hrs Hamilton received a 'Secret and Most Immediate' message from London: 'Cruiser Force to withdraw to westward at high speed.' Twelve minutes later the Admiralty sent Broome a signal: 'Owing to threat from surface ships convoy is to disperse and proceed to Russian ports.' The Admiralty discovered the Kriegsmarine heavy units were no longer at Trondheim, Narvik or Vestfjord. The Admiralty assumed they were at sea, intercepting PQ-17. Thirteen minutes later Broome received another signal ordering the convoy to scatter. Assuming this meant *Tirpitz* was close, Broome and Hamilton reluctantly followed orders.

The Survivors

After PQ-17 dispersed, the merchant ships' escorts abandoned them under Admiralty orders to prevent the convoy from reforming. One captain, Lt Leo Gradwell, RNVR, commanding the antisubmarine trawler HMS *Ayrshire*, disregarded the order. Finding steamship *Ironclad* heading north, he began escorting it and the pair soon encountered *Troubadour*, another old Hog Islander, like *Ironclad*.

It joined them as Gradwell took his charges to the edge of the pack ice where they found another Hog Islander, *Silver Sword*, skirting the ice pack and which joined the other three ships. Gradwell led his unlikely convoy into the ice, breaking the way for the freighters until they were 25 miles into the ice pack and could go no further.

All three freighters were coal-burners, and *Troubadour*'s cargo included bunker coal, intended for Russia. It also carried a large quantity of white paint. Gradwell decided their best strategy would be to lie hidden in the ice long enough for the Germans to stop searching for ships from the scattered convoy. He ordered the boiler fires banked, both to save fuel and eliminate smoke.

To increase the ships' concealment, Gradwell ordered *Troubadour*'s white paint distributed. Crews painted all visible metal surfaces white: *Troubadour* and *Ayrshire* enthusiastically slathered white paint on both sides of their ships, whereas *Ironclad* and *Silver Sword* only coated their starboard sides with paint, exposed as they were to searching Germans. Surfaces that could not be painted, such as hatch covers, were covered with white bedsheets and table linen.

Additionally, *Troubadour* and *Ironside* had deck cargoes of M-3 tanks which Gradwell authorized opened, and their guns manned. Their 37mm turret cannon would augment the ships' antiaircraft batteries if they were discovered. German aircraft flew by them while they were so hidden, but missed seeing them.

The ships remained in the ice for three days, finally emerging on 7 July. By then, the hunt was dying down and Gradwell took his charges to Novaya Zemlya, from where they safely reached Arkhangelsk. Gradwell would be awarded the Distinguished Service Cross for his actions. A barrister before the war, Gradwell resumed his profession at war's end, ultimately becoming a magistrate.

This plate captures these survivors on 5 July, balanced between safety and peril. They are hidden in the ice, 20 miles in from the pack edge, and have camouflaged their ships with white paint, table linens and sheets. Their fires are banked, so they are making no smoke. In the distance a scouting German Blohm & Voss BV 138, a 'flying clog' due to its distinctive profile, reconnoitres along the edge of the ice, seeking ships sheltering there.

The men aboard the four ships hold their collective breaths. Will they be spotted? The crew of the BV 138 seek what they expect – ships hiding along the pack edge. They are probably tired, since it is a long trip from their Bodö anchorage to the summer ice limit, and never dream their prey is so deep into the ice pack. They fly on, never detecting what is hidden in plain sight.

The convoy began dispersing, sending ships on pre-determined courses independently of each other. Broome attached his destroyers to the Cruiser Force, intending to join them in battling the Kriegsmarine. The slower escorts, the trawlers, corvettes and antiaircraft ships, joined the scatter plan. In actuality, *Tirpitz* and its companions were then moored in Altenfjord, but by the time this was known, the dispersal could not be undone.

Palomares gathered a minesweeper and trawler as an escort, and steamed towards Russia. Two corvettes steamed independently to Arkhangelsk. *Pozarica* asked permission to escort seven freighters in a mini-convoy, but this was denied. Instead, it steamed to Arkhangelsk with two corvettes. None of these warships were molested during their voyages. The merchant ships were more attractive targets.

Only one warship disregarded orders, the trawler *Aryshire*. Its captain, Leo Gradwell, a Royal Navy Volunteer Reserve officer from New Zealand, headed north, instead of steaming directly to Arkhangelsk. He collected three freighters heading north due to the scatter order, Panamanian *Troubadour*, British *Ironclad* and US *Silver Sword*, and led the ships deep into the ice pack. There, Gradwell had them bank their fires and wait. Using white paint aboard *Troubador*, tablecloths and sheets, they camouflaged the ships. Some of the ships were carrying M-3 tanks and their crews broke into them and loaded the guns, intending to use their 37mm guns as antiaircraft guns. Then they waited until the hunt died down. In the event, the guns proved unnecessary as scouting aircraft missed them in the ice.

For the rest of the transports, the next few days were a nightmare. The Luftwaffe and U-boats tore into them. *Pan Kraft* died first, disabled by high-level bombing, then strafed and set blazing by a Ju 88. By 1500hrs on 5 July, all three squadrons of KG 30 were quartering the Barents Sea, hunting merchantmen. Ju 88s bombed and sank *Fairfield City* as it was sailing in company with *Daniel Morgan* which ducked into mist. Five Ju 88s caught up with *Daniel Morgan* later, sinking it, too. Ju 88s found the munitions-laden British *Earlston*. Brought to a halt when near-misses damaged its engine, it was abandoned, and then sunk by a U-boat.

Seven He 111s came across US-flag *Peter Kerr*. They sent 14 torpedoes at it, all of which missed. Then four Ju 88s dropped a dozen bombs on it of which three hit, setting it ablaze. It exploded shortly after the crew abandoned it.

El Capitan (shown in pre-war days) was one of the PQ-17 freighters falling prey to the Luftwaffe after dispersal. It was fatally wounded by Ju 88s bombs on 9 July after departing Novaya Zemlya for Arkhangelsk. (USNHHC)

Four freighters, *Paulus Potter*, *Bolton Castle*, *Olopana* and *Washington* set off together. The elderly *Olopana* fell behind and the other three were found and attacked by Ju 88s. *Bolton Castle* and *Washington* were sunk by the bombers, and *Paulus Potter* was crippled, allowing *U-255* to finish it. *U-255* then sank the straggling *Olopana* two days later. *Aldersdale*, *Earlston*, *Empire Byron* and *William Hooper* were also crippled by aircraft in the 24 hours after dispersal and finished off by U-boats. Seven other merchantmen from PQ-17 were hunted down and sunk by U-boats alone.

What was left of the convoy reconstituted itself at Novaya Zemlya, where the survivors fled for safety, before steaming as a group to Arkhangelsk. *El Capitan* almost made it to safety but was caught by a Ju 88 as it neared the White Sea. Damaged, it was abandoned, and later sunk by *U-251*. Only 13 freighters made it to port safely, including the three shepherded by *Ayrshire*. Of these, one ran aground off Novaya Zemlya, and was later refloated. *Ayrshire* and its three charges arrived at Arkhangelsk on 20 July, last by a week of all the survivors, except for *Azerbaijan*, to make port. *Azerbaijan* arrived on the same day as the other four, having survived an air attack before the convoy dispersed, and the trek across the Barents afterwards.

QP-13 did not reach port intact either. On 5 July its Reykjavík-bound ships hit fog and, due to a navigation error, they sailed into an Allied minefield off Iceland. Five ships struck 'friendly' mines, and four sank.

PQ-17's survivors under escort from Novaya Zemlya to Arkhangelsk. The antiaircraft ship *Pozarica* or *Palomares* is on the left, to the right of it (in order) are *Silver Sword*, *Ironclad* and a Russian ship. The photo was taken from *Troubadour*. (USNHHC)

The Empire strikes back: 21 July–30 September 1942

The PQ-17 disaster, for that is what it was, had consequences reverberating until the end of the war. The first and most immediate was the cancellation of further convoys during the summer months. The combined risk posed by Kriegsmarine surface ships, plus U-boats and Luftwaffe aircraft, was viewed as too great during the long summer nights and the next convoys would not depart until September. Two other consequences were also immediate: PQ-17 caused the morale of merchant mariners manning civilian ships to plummet, and encouraged the Luftwaffe to redouble efforts against Arctic convoys.

In August 1942 Britain increased its aircraft presence in northern Russia, sending Hampden torpedo bombers and Catalina maritime patrol aircraft to assist Arctic convoys. Catalinas, like the one shown, provided protection from U-boats on the voyage's final leg. (Wikimedia Commons)

Merchant marine sailors felt betrayed by the Royal Navy's abandonment of PQ-17. They were told the fast escorts were needed to fight off an imminent surface attack, which they sort of understood, but the refusal of the corvettes, minesweepers, antiaircraft ships and ASW trawlers (except *Ayrshire*) to provide protection was seen as unforgivable. Especially since the remaining escorts formed groups of antisubmarine warfare vessels and antiaircraft vessels, maximizing the chances they would survive. They simultaneously refused to allow civilian ships to accompany them because of Admiralty orders that civilian ships were to disperse. It made it seem as though the Royal Navy was only interested in its own safety, not that of the merchant marine. The disregard was more pointed due to the example of *Ayrshire*, which successfully brought its charges to safety. The crews manning PQ-18's ships lacked confidence in their protectors.

The Luftwaffe, however, assumed the dispersal had been triggered by their attacks on 4 July. It occurred after a long day of almost continuous attacks in which they had taken losses, especially among Ju 88s, but the long hiatus allowed most losses to be replaced and, in some cases, Gruppes were reinforced. By the time the next convoy sailed, 87 Ju 88s were stationed at Banak and Bardufoss, of which 35 were capable of carrying torpedoes. There were also 46 He 111 and 15 He 115s operating out of Finnmark airfields. Furthermore, these could be supplemented by Ju 87s operating out of Kirkenes if a convoy ventured too near the Scandinavian coasts.

For scouting, BV 138s of Küstenfliegergruppe 906 were available, as were the reconnaissance Fw 200s and Ju 88s of KG 40. In a pinch, the KG 40 aircraft could attack ships, especially those sailing individually due to straggling or if the Luftwaffe forced the convoy to dispersion.

Finally, Bf 109 fighters of Jagdgeschwader 5 were available to provide fighter cover for the bombers if reports an aircraft carrier would accompany the convoy were true. This was dependent on operations occurring close to the coast, however. The Bf 109 was short-ranged and would mainly see use protecting the bomber bases from air attack.

Regardless of the Luftwaffe, Britain was eager to resume Arctic convoys – with appropriate preparation this time. Defence would be an all-British effort, as the US ships on loan from May through July were needed elsewhere (*Washington* went to the Pacific, where in November it would fight a duel with the Japanese battleship *Kirishima*). However, Britain could make up that shortfall.

The first step was re-equipping the escorts of the next homeward-bound convoy. They were low on ammunition, and their antiaircraft guns worn out. Four destroyers loaded with ammunition and spare gun barrels for *Palomares* and *Pozarica* arrived in Arkhangelsk on 24 July. They also carried German-speaking interpreters for the antiaircraft ships; to provide real-time intelligence, as had been done aboard *Alynbank* in PQ-16.

But greater airpower was needed. The Soviets finally gave permission for RAF units to operate out of Russian airfields and two squadrons of Hampden torpedo bombers, a Catalina patrol squadron and a flight of photo-reconnaissance Spitfires were relocated to Kola Peninsula airfields. A task force with US heavy cruiser *Tuscaloosa*, two US destroyers and a Royal Navy destroyer left Glasgow for the Kola Inlet on 13 August. Aboard were the ground crew, stores and equipment for these Coastal Command squadrons. The aircraft flew in later, after their bases were established. These aircraft were primarily intended as a check on Kriegsmarine surface units, and were operational when September started.

Furthermore, to provide local air cover, an escort carrier was assigned to the next convoy. *Avenger* was a merchant conversion built in the US, provided to the Royal Navy through Lend-Lease. It carried three radar-equipped Swordfish for antisubmarine protection and 12 Sea Hurricane Mk IBs, for air defence. It was accompanied by two dedicated destroyers, for protection during launch and landing operations, when it had to leave the convoy.

The *Avenger*'s presence had a second beneficial effect. The Germans had learned a carrier would accompany the convoy when they captured plans aboard a Hampden, downed flying to Russia, and Göring ordered his aircraft to prioritize sinking the carrier. Merchant ships were to be ignored until the carrier was sunk and this meant they were attacked significantly less in the battle's opening stages.

The outbound convoy, designated PQ-18, would contain 39 merchantmen, a rescue ship, three RFA oilers, and three minesweepers to be turned over to the Soviet Navy. These minesweepers served as rescue ships during the trip, and one merchantmen was CAM ship

The Dido-class light cruisers, built as antiaircraft ships, had a main battery of heavy antiaircraft guns (either 5.25in or 4.5in), advanced radar (note the antennae on the mast) and a sophisticated combat information centre to coordinate air defence. HMS *Scylla*, a Dido-class cruiser, accompanied PQ-18. (AC)

Empire Morn. The convoy carried 235,00grt of cargo capacity and departed from Loch Ewe, Scotland. The homeward-bound convoy, QP-14, had 17 merchantmen of 97,000grt, including survivors of PQ-17 and some from PQ-16 (one was CAM ship *Empire Tide*), and it departed from Arkhangelsk.

The escorts for these convoys were the heaviest yet. Close escort for PQ-18 was two destroyers, two antiaircraft ships, two submarines, four corvettes, three minesweepers and four trawlers. It would also be accompanied by *Avenger* and its two destroyers. Also accompanying PQ-18 would be a 'fighting destroyer escort', antiaircraft cruiser *Scylla* and 16 destroyers. These were intended as a substitute for a cruiser force east of Bear Island since the Royal Navy wished to keep its heavy units west of Bear Island due to the difficulty of repair if they were damaged east of it. They recognized a need to protect convoys from German heavy surface units east of 20 degrees East and an escort of 16 torpedo-armed destroyers was viewed as a match for any combination of Kriegsmarine heavy cruisers. They provided a second major benefit: increasing the convoy's antiaircraft defences.

QP-14 had a close escort made up of antiaircraft ships *Palomares* and *Pozarica*, one destroyer, four corvettes, three minesweepers and four trawlers. It would be joined by the fighting destroyer escort when the convoys crossed paths.

There would also be a Cruiser Covering Force made up of three heavy cruisers to shield convoys west of Bear Island and to protect Spitzbergen-bound ships. The Allies were sending two cruisers and one destroyer to carry supplies and reinforcements to Spitzbergen, as well as two fleet oilers protected by four destroyers to refuel them. This force was being sent so a necessary operation at Spitzbergen would occur when the Germans were busy with PQ-18 and QP-14.

Finally, to guard against the possibility of *Tirpitz* breaking out, there was a distant covering force of *Anson*, *Duke of York*, a light cruiser and five destroyers. It had no aircraft carrier as *Victorious* was undergoing a refit.

PQ-18 left Loch Ewe on 2 September bound for Reykjavík in Iceland. It immediately ran into a storm, which disrupted the convoy, and although U-boats picked up the convoy in the Atlantic they were driven off. PQ-18 rounded the southwest corner of Iceland on 7 September. On 8 September, PQ-18 was found by a Condor, which subsequently lost it in fog.

Three days earlier, *Avenger* and her destroyers were attacked by another Condor, while waiting at Seidisfjord to join PQ-18. The bombs missed, but the sighting alerted the Germans

Near midday on 12 September, a BV 138 reconnaissance aircraft dropped out of the overcast, spotting the convoy. After that PQ-18 was under virtually continuous aerial observation. (AC)

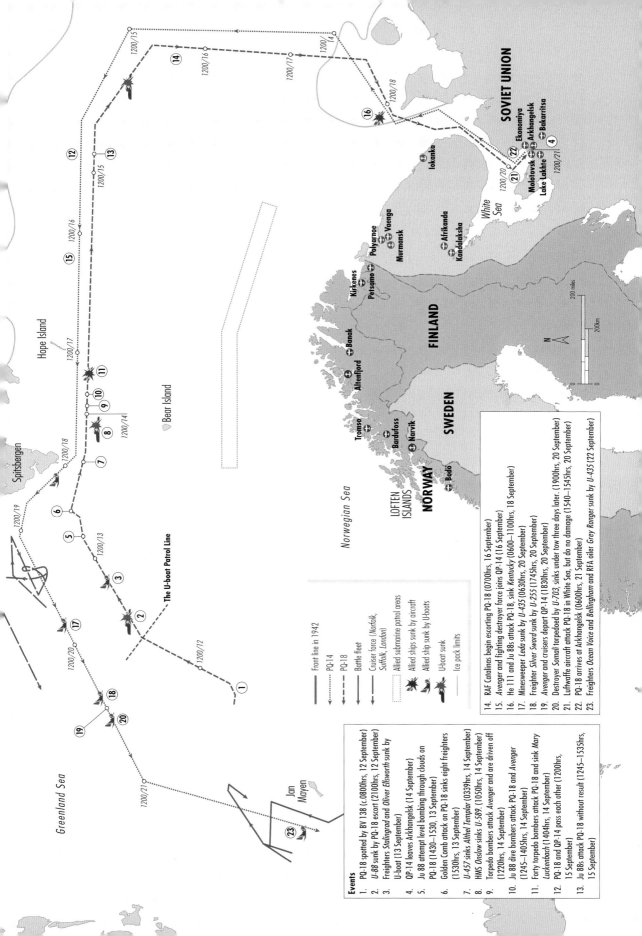

Greenland Sea

Jan
Mayen

Spitsbergen

Hope Island

Bear Island

Norwegian Sea

NORWAY

LOFOTEN
ISLANDS

Bodö

Narvik
Bardufoss
Tromsø

SWEDEN

FINLAND

Altenfjord

Banak

Kirkenes
Petsamo

Polyarnoe
Vaenga
Murmansk

Afrikanda
Kandalaksha

Iokanka

White
Sea

SOVIET UNION

Ekonomiya
Arkhangelsk
Molotovsk
Lake Lakhte
Bakaritsa

N

0   200km
0   200 miles

The U-boat Patrol Line

Events

1. PQ-18 spotted by BV 138 (c.0800hrs, 12 September)
2. *U-88* sunk by PQ-18 escort (2100hrs, 12 September)
3. Freighters *Stalingrad* and *Oliver Ellsworth* sunk by U-boat (13 September)
4. QP-14 leaves Arkhangelsk (14 September)
5. Ju 88 attempt level bombing through clouds on PQ-18 (1430–1530, 13 September)
6. Golden Comb attack on PQ-18 sinks eight freighters (1530hrs, 13 September)
7. *U-457* sinks *Athel Templar* (0339hrs, 14 September)
8. HMS *Onslow* sinks *U-589*. (1050hrs, 14 September)
9. Torpedo bombers attack *Avenger* and are driven off (1220hrs, 14 September)
10. Ju 88 dive bombers attack PQ-18 and *Avenger* (1245–1405hrs, 14 September)
11. Forty torpedo bombers attack PQ-18 and sink *Mary Luckenbach* (1404hrs, 14 September)
12. PQ-18 and QP-14 pass each other (1200hrs, 15 September)
13. Ju 88s attack PQ-18 without result (1245–1535hrs, 15 September)
14. RAF Catalinas begin escorting PQ-18 (0700hrs, 16 September)
15. *Avenger* and fighting destroyer force joins QP-14 (16 September)
16. He 111 and Ju 88s attack PQ-18, sink *Kentucky* (0600–1100hrs, 18 September)
17. Minesweeper *Leda* sunk by *U-435* (0630hrs, 20 September)
18. Freighter *Silver Sword* sunk by *U-255* (1745hrs, 20 September)
19. *Avenger* and cruisers depart QP-14 (1830hrs, 20 September)
20. Destroyer *Somali* torpedoed by *U-703*, sinks under tow three days later. (1900hrs, 20 September)
21. Luftwaffe aircraft attack PQ-18 in White Sea, but do no damage (1540–1545hrs, 20 September)
22. PQ-18 arrives at Arkhangelsk (0600hrs, 21 September)
23. Freighters *Ocean Voice* and *Bellingham* and RFA oiler *Grey Ranger* sunk by *U-435* (22 September)

Front line in 1942
PQ-14
PQ-18
Battle fleet
Cruiser force (*Norfolk*, *Suffolk*, *London*)
Allied submarine patrol areas
Allied ships sunk by aircraft
Allied ship sunk by U-boats
U-boat sunk
Ice pack limits

In addition to 12 Sea Hurricanes, *Avenger* carried three radar-equipped Swordfish. Intended for ASW duties, the biplane Swordfish sparred with the Luftwaffe aircraft attacking PQ-18. Generally this occurred when the German bombers found opportunities to protect U-boats attacked by Swordfish. (AC)

a carrier would be with the convoy. German intelligence evaluated the ship sent as *Argus*, an elderly carrier dating to World War I. *Avenger* left Seidisfjord on 8 September, joining PQ-18 the following day.

PQ-18 steamed east, avoiding further detection until 12 September when day brought a low overcast, with clear skies below the clouds. A BV 138 dropped out of the overcast, spotting the convoy. *Avenger* launched Hurricanes, but they failed to find their shadower. At 2100hrs, *U-88* came across the convoy, but was promptly sunk.

The next day found PQ-18 almost continuously shadowed by BV 138s and reconnaissance Ju 88s. They helped direct U-boats to the convoy while *Avenger*'s Swordfish attempted to keep the U-boats submerged, but the BV-138s and Ju 88s attacked the Swordfish and were reported dropping mines ahead of the convoy. *Avenger* launched Hurricanes to drive off the aircraft but again they failed to make contact. Meanwhile, *U-589* torpedoed and sank the Soviet freighter *Stalingrad* and Liberty Ship *Oliver Ellsworth*.

QP-14 left Arkhangelsk on 13 September, its close escort accompanied by four minesweepers for the first 48 hours at sea. Since German attention was focused on PQ-18, it went undetected until 20 September, four days after the convoys passed.

Things only got worse for PQ-18 as 13 September continued. The destroyers and *Scylla*, which broke off to refuel during the morning, rejoined the convoy at 1420. Over the next hour, Ju 88s made level bombing attempts through holes in the clouds, and at 1520, radar from the antiaircraft ships and *Avenger* picked up a massive incoming raid: 37 mid-level Ju 88s followed by low-level torpedo bombers, 28 He 111s and 18 Ju 88s. *Avenger*'s Hurricanes however were on or approaching the carrier, low on fuel after having interfered with the previous attacks.

Twenty Ju 88s attacked first, coming in at medium altitude, to draw attention from the torpedo aircraft. Meanwhile, the torpedo aircraft themselves formed a wide line abreast approaching the convoy from one side and ahead. They were led by a reconnaissance Ju 88, which had broken away from PQ-18 to guide in the torpedo bombers. They were launching the war's first Golden Comb attack.

They went undetected during the first critical minutes of their attack. The convoy commodore ordered a 45-degree turn to port, a signal missed by the convoy's two right-hand columns, closest to the attackers. A belated wall of antiaircraft fire came out from the convoy to stop the torpedo bombers, but a line of over 80 torpedoes streaked towards the convoy. Eight ships were hit and sunk, most from the columns that failed to alter course. Only five bombers were shot down.

The German success caused a shift in *Avenger*'s air coverage. Instead of pursuing shadowing aircraft, the Hurricanes were kept aloft to attack and break up bomber formations. To ensure continuous coverage, Hurricanes flew aloft in pairs or trios, staying airborne for 25 minutes before landing to refuel. While they would not shoot down many aircraft, they could prevent attacks from forming unmolested.

At 0330hrs on 14 September, *U-457* torpedoed the tanker *Athel Templar*, which was subsequently scuttled. Revenge was gained when an ASW Swordfish detected a surfaced U-boat, and although the 'Stringbag' was driven off by a recon Ju 88, it marked the submarine's location with a smoke float. A destroyer, HMS *Onslow*, later found and sank *U-589* at 1050hrs. Combat between Swordfish and BV 138s and Ju 88s continued throughout the morning and into early afternoon.

Death of the *Mary Luckenbach*

The most spectacular casualty of Convoy PQ-18 was steamship *Mary Luckenbach*. It was one of several dozen vessels owned by the New York City-based Luckenbach Steamship Co., all of which were named after different members of the owning family. In 1942 most of the company's vessels were ships built between 1916 and 1920 for the Emergency Fleet Corporation to augment World War I shipping. Most were sold as surplus in the 1920s. The Luckenbach Line filled its interwar fleet with these large, well-built, cheap and new ships in the 1920s, buying up older ones in good condition thereafter.

This included *Mary Luckenbach*, purchased in 1941. Assigned to PQ-18, *Mary Luckenbach* was in column nine of the convoy during the Golden Comb attack on 13 September, and was the only ship in column nine or ten to survive the attack.

The next day, the Luftwaffe renewed its attack on PQ-18. Directives from the Luftwaffe's commander, Hermann Göring, made the escort carrier *Avenger* the bombers' main target. At about 1420hrs a wave of He 111 torpedo bombers swept in, flying over the convoy to attack *Avenger*. *Mary Luckenbach* was then in column seven, the next-to-last column on the right. One He 111, perhaps injured by antiaircraft fire, dropped its torpedoes before nearing *Avenger*, and one of these hit *Mary Luckenbach*, which carried 1,000 tons of TNT in its cargo.

What happened? Observers differ on events leading up to its destruction, but Ensign Daniel Rooke, with the gun crews aboard freighter *Campfire*, reported driving off three aircraft heading towards them. Two swerved over *Mary Luckenbach*, dropping their loads on it. One was blown up with the ship.

Lieutenant John Landers, aboard *Virginia Dare*, wrote: '... six [He 111's] came madly down the columns between ships towards our end of the convoy, flying only 20 to 30 feet above the water and hopping in a peculiar fashion. One plane came in a little abaft the starboard beam. The plane turned slightly and headed for the *Mary Luckenbach*; released its torpedoes, tried to gain elevation, and then crashed. The *Luckenbach* blew up.'

Others reported the He 111 strafed *Luckenbach* as it passed over the ship, and some claim the aircraft torpedoing *Luckenbach* crashed half a mile after exiting the convoy. But everyone agreed what happened next. Vice Admiral Boddam-Whetham described the event: 'She [*Mary Luckenbach*] completely detonated. A huge cloud of black and grey smoke went up to the cloud base and there mushroomed out.'

This plate attempts to recreate the last few seconds of *Mary Luckenbach*'s existence. It shows the He 111 that torpedoed *Mary Luckenbach* passing over it, firing and being fired upon. The aircraft was almost certainly fatally damaged at that point, dropping its torpedoes at a foe it could reach before crashing. A second He 111, still carrying its two torpedoes is passing behind *Mary Luckenbach*, intent on reaching *Avenger*. Within 15 seconds one of the two torpedoes dropped will strike home, creating an explosion with enough force to leave the ships surrounding *Mary Luckenbach* convinced they had also been torpedoed.

PQ-18's most spectacular casualty was *Mary Luckenbach*, shown here in happier pre-war days. A torpedo detonated 1,000 tons of TNT on board, resulting in a literal 1 kiloton explosion. (AC)

Shortly after noon, Swordfish detected a swarm of incoming torpedo bombers and from 12 to 20 torpedo-armed Ju 88s attacked *Avenger*. The convoy wheeled 45 degrees to avoid them. *Avenger* had Hurricanes aloft, and turned to avoid the torpedo bombers while its attendant destroyers put up a curtain of antiaircraft fire. They were joined by *Scylla* and *Ulster Queen*, which broke formation to protect *Avenger*. The barrage broke up the attack; 11 aircraft were shot down and the torpedo bombers scored no hits. At 1245hrs, Ju 88 dive bombers appeared. Over the next 80 minutes they made futile attacks on *Avenger* and its escorts, managing only near-misses on *Avenger* and two destroyers which did little damage. One bomber was shot down.

At 1405hrs another raid of 40 torpedo bombers, 22 He 111s and 18 Ju 88s went after the convoy. Most went after *Avenger*, flying over the convoy to do so. They were met by four Sea Hurricanes and a ferocious antiaircraft barrage. The combination broke up the attack and five bombers were shot down, with another nine so badly damaged they were unserviceable for the rest of the battle. Three Hurricanes were shot down, all by 'friendly fire' but all three pilots were recovered. *Avenger* avoided the few torpedoes fired at it, though one torpedo struck *Mary Luckenbach* which, loaded with ammunition, exploded.

Another hour of half-hearted dive bombing attacks followed, but no further damage was done. At 1530hrs the last KG 30 Ju 88 climbed into the clouds and headed home. That day, reconnaissance reported *Tirpitz* absent from its moorings and although 23 Hampdens were scrambled to search for it, they found nothing. *Tirpitz* was not at sea, but on an exercise in another fjord.

15 September dawned with calm seas and a cloud ceiling at 3,000ft. Swordfish began antisubmarine patrols at dawn, shadowers found PQ-18 at 0800hrs and the first bombers began arriving shortly after noon. Three hours of attacks followed. This time the demoralized Luftwaffe crews circled, occasionally, but only tentatively attacking. At 1645hrs, they gave up and flew home having scored no hits and losing one Ju 88 to radar-controlled gunnery fired through clouds.

The next day, PQ-18 came within range of Russian-base RAF Catalinas, which relieved *Avenger*'s Swordfish of ASW patrols. In the morning, PQ-18's escort sank *U-457*, and that afternoon they exchanged signals with QP-14. Over the next few hours, *Avenger* and the fighting destroyer force left PQ-18 in groups to join QP-14.

PQ-18 continued undisturbed until it neared Russia on 18 September. By then its diminished escort had been joined by four Soviet destroyers. Twelve KG 26 He 111s, the only ones left available, with some dive-bombing Ju 88s, attacked the convoy. A torpedo hit and sank 5,446grt *Kentucky*. Tugs from *Iokanka* tried to tow *Kentucky* to harbour, but a Ju 88 landed two bombs on the freighter, and the fires attracted more bombers. *Empire Morn* launched its Hurricat, which set one of the He 111 afire. The Hurricat pilot then set course for Keg Ostrov airfield, where he landed safely. Although near-misses damaged some ships, *Kentucky* was the last ship lost before PQ-18 reached Arkhangelsk on 21 September.

QP-14, fortunate through the first part of its voyage, was less so in the last half. *Avenger*, *Scylla* and much of the destroyer escort intended for defence against aircraft and warships departed on 20 and 21 September. Without *Avenger*'s Swordfish, PQ-14 lost an important part of its anti-U-boat protection. The U-boats, largely impotent against PQ-18, suddenly proved deadly to QP-14, sinking three freighters, RFA oiler *Grey Ranger*, minesweeper *Leda* and Tribal-class destroyer *Somali* between 20 September and 22 September.

While the latest round of convoys was not the utter defeat of PQ-17/QP-13, it was not the clear victory for which the British had hoped. Of the 56 merchant bottoms leaving port, 16 failed to reach port, including a good third of the stores-carrying PQ-18. Additionally, two warships and an RFA tanker were lost. German losses, though, were high. During the battles for the two convoys the Luftwaffe lost 33 He 111 and Ju 88 torpedo bombers, six Ju 88 dive bombers and two long-range reconnaissance aircraft. With 337 sorties flown that amounted to a 13 per cent loss rate. The Kriegsmarine lost four U-boats, all lost fighting PQ-18.

Murmansk improved throughout the war. By 1944 more cranes facilitated unloading, more warehouses were added and transportation links expanded. This increased Murmansk's cargo capacity. (USNHHC)

Three more years of war: 1 October 1942–30 May 1945

There was no PQ-19, although by the end of September 40 ships had been assembled for it. Other theatres, especially the North African landings scheduled for early November, required the escort carriers, antiaircraft ships (especially the auxiliary antiaircraft cruisers) and fleet destroyers necessary for a successful Arctic convoy. On 22 September, Churchill told Roosevelt no further Arctic convoys could be made until January.

Roosevelt called this 'a tough blow for the Russians', and urged PQ-19 be run as a succession of smaller convoys. Informed this could be done only by postponing the North African landings three weeks, Roosevelt reluctantly agreed to the postponement. Stalin was not so easily placated. The struggle for Stalingrad was approaching a climax and he demanded ships be sent anyway. Earlier, at his insistence, in August, two Russian freighters, *Friedrich Engles* and *Belomorcanal*, sailed independently from Iceland to Arkhangelsk. Departing a day apart on 11 and 12 August, both arrived successfully.

To placate Stalin, Britain instituted Operation *FB* in late October. Starting on 29 October ships began sailing individually from Iceland at 12-hour intervals. By then, it was almost completely dark throughout the day in the Arctic regions these ships would pass through. There were a few hours of twilight around noon, a period which shrank as each day passed, and it was hoped that darkness would provide sufficient protection.

Some crews were offered cash bonuses, paid in advance, to participate, and 13 ships departed Iceland over the next week. Of these, three turned back to Iceland, three were sunk by U-boats, one by a Luftwaffe aircraft, one wrecked on Spitzbergen and five reached Arkhangelsk. Another 23 vessels, largely Russian-flagged ships, sailed independently from Russia during this period. These were more successful and only one was sunk; 22 others arrived safely at Iceland.

The Catalina squadron was recalled from Russia in early October, following the arrival of QP-14. Dido-class antiaircraft cruiser *Argonaut* and two destroyers steamed for Arkhangelsk on 13 October. Delivering a portable hospital to treat wounded merchant mariners, they returned the RAF aircrew and ground personnel from the two Hampden squadrons and the photo-recon unit to Britain. The surviving bombers and Spitfires were turned over to the Soviets. Although reconnaissance aircraft spotted these warships, Luftwaffe aircraft did not attack them during their passage.

Operation *Torch*, the landings in northwest Africa, began on 7 November. It involved over 500 transports and cargo vessels, temporarily absorbing most of the Home Fleet during the month preceding and following the landings. As an immediate consequence, Luftflotte 5, including the torpedo bombers of KG 26 and the dive bombers of KG 30, were transferred to the Mediterranean. This left only 15 torpedo-carrying He 115s, a dozen or so KG 30 Ju 88s, around three dozen Ju 87s and a handful of maritime patrol aircraft in Norway and Lapland. The slow He 115s were adequate for picking off individual stragglers, but were incapable of attacking a well-defended convoy without suffering prohibitive losses. The Stukas lacked the range necessary for threatening convoys except when they neared the Kola Inlet, and by late 1942 Soviet fighter defences around Murmansk made that risky. However, air raids on Murmansk would continue to sink or damage merchant ships in the Kola Inlet through 1944.

Taking the opportunity offered by the sudden lack of enemy aircraft, a convoy, QP-15, was hastily organized to return the many ships sitting empty at Arkhangelsk. It consisted of 32 merchant vessels, 25 of which survived PQ-18. Several failed to sail or returned to port, and only 28 attempted the passage to Iceland. Its close escort consisted of four corvettes and a minesweeper. Once at sea it was joined by *Ulster Queen* and five destroyers. Distant cover, intended to protect it from Kriegsmarine warships once it was west of Bear Island, was provided by two cruisers and three destroyers.

It left Arkhangelsk on 15 November, with two Soviet destroyers accompanying it during the first two days out of port. Winter storms began buffeting the convoy almost as soon as

it left, and continued through much of its passage. The weather was so bad that it sank one Russian destroyer, scattered the convoy and kept the ocean escort destroyers from finding the merchantmen. It also kept Luftwaffe reconnaissance grounded and Kriegsmarine surface warships in port. Two transports were found and sunk by U-boats, but the other 26 straggled safely into Loch Ewe between 30 November and 3 December.

The Luftwaffe withdrawal from the north was intended to be temporary, with Luftflotte 5 returning in spring 1943, to take advantage of the long Arctic days. Losses incurred in the Mediterranean during the winter of 1942–43 and the aerial resupply of Wehrmacht forces isolated in Stalingrad however made this impossible. The surviving aircraft were needed elsewhere. Bomber production was slashed in mid-1943, which left too few replacements to build up bomber numbers sufficiently to allow more aircraft to be sent to Finnmark.

Not until the autumn of 1944 did the Luftwaffe return to Finnmark airfields, when two much-diminished Gruppes of KG 26 transferred back to Banak and Bardufoss. The transfer was due less to renewed interest in Arctic convoys than necessity. With airfields in French Atlantic regions overrun, and the Mediterranean an Allied lake, Norway was the sole remaining German-held territory relevant to torpedo bombers. The battles over Arctic convoys were not over, but it was largely fought only by Kriegsmarine warships and U-boats, aided primarily by Luftwaffe reconnaissance. It was enough to pose a threat to convoys, but not enough to create serious casualties.

Convoys resumed in December 1942. For security reasons – or maybe from a sense that the old system was jinxed – the Russian-bound convoys were prefixed by JW and the homeward convoys RA. Additionally, the numbering for both started with 51, and continued sequentially. Rather than send one big convoy, the 30 ships intended for JW-51 was split into two parts, JW-51A with 16 merchant vessels and JW-51B with 14.

JW-51A, departing 15 December 1942, slipped through undetected, arriving at Kola Inlet without loss on Christmas Day. JW-51B, which departed 22 December, was challenged by *Lützow* and *Hipper*. In a battle fought on New Year's Eve, they were driven away by two British light cruisers. The convoy arrived at Kola Inlet on 4 January 1943 without loss. One ship, *Ballot*, was however lost by shipwreck a week after arrival. Homebound RA-51 left Kola Inlet with 14 merchantmen on 30 December 1942, arriving at Loch Ewe on 11 January, also without loss.

The New Year's Eve battle resulted in a shakeup at the Kriegsmarine. Raeder stepped down, to be replaced as head of the Kriegsmarine by Karl Dönitz. Over the next two years Dönitz would prove less successful wielding the Kriegsmarine against Arctic convoys than Raeder had been during his eighteen months.

Two more JW convoys and a pair of RA convoys sailed in January and February. The 41 ships of the two JW convoys arrived without loss. The ten ships of RA-52 similarly arrived

Starting with Convoy JW-57 in February 1944, every Arctic convoy included one or two British escort carriers. These were used mainly for protection against U-boats as Luftwaffe bombers were absent from the Arctic during 1944 and present only in small numbers thereafter. (AC)

at Loch Ewe without loss, while three of the 30 homebound ships in RA-53 were sunk by U-boats during its two-week voyage. A fourth, *J. L. M. Curry*, broke up in an Arctic storm, and sank. (It was one of three Liberty ships lost through low-temperature hull steel embrittlement.) Only one ship was sunk by aircraft, the 7,173grt *Ocean Freedom* was sunk in port two weeks after arrival.

These convoys were better protected than the 1942 convoys. The merchant ships travelling were increasingly of war construction, with heavy antiaircraft batteries. The ocean escorts also included one or sometimes two Dido-class antiaircraft cruisers and destroyers with improved and radar-controlled antiaircraft batteries. When a dozen Ju 88s tested these antiaircraft defences during RA-53, they were met with a barrage so fierce they broke off the attack.

After RA-53, 1943 sailings were suspended until well after the autumnal equinox, resuming on 1 November, when RA-54 sailed. It was followed by seven more convoys, four outbound and three homebound which sailed before 1943 ended and another eight, four each way, which sailed between 1 January 1944 and 7 April 1944. Only five ships in these convoys were lost, all to U-boats and all in 1944.

These convoys were not without drama. *Tirpitz* had been disabled in September 1943 and remained out of action until finally sunk in November 1944. *Scharnhorst*, Germany's sole remaining capital ship attempted to attack JW-55B in December 1944, but instead, on Boxing Day, 26 December, it was sunk in a duel with *Duke of York*. The surviving Kriegsmarine surface warships never again challenged an Arctic convoy.

Most importantly, every convoy starting with JW-57 had one or two escort carriers as part of the ocean escort. They carried ASW Swordfish, and initially Grumman Martlet/Wildcat fighters. The Swordfish helped neutralize U-boat attacks; the Martlets were too slow to catch reconnaissance Ju 88s, but were capable of breaking up any air attacks on convoys. They, unlike earlier Sea Hurricanes, could and did shoot down any snoopers venturing too close.

Arctic escort carriers had Wildcat fighters aboard. The fighters' 0.50cal machine guns were capable of quickly destroying any Luftwaffe aircraft attacking a convoy, but they were too slow to catch fleeing German aircraft. Regardless, they prevented the Luftwaffe from attacking convoys and drove off aerial scouts. (AC)

Convoys were again suspended after April, to resume on 15 August 1944. Part of the reason was the shipping demands of the Normandy landings in northern France which sucked up every spare cargo ship. Between August 1944 and the surrender of Germany on 7 May 1945, 18 convoys made the Arctic run, nine each way. A final pair departed in May, after the surrender. Thereafter, convoys were permanently suspended, with ships sailing individually, and lighted, under peacetime conditions. Nine ships were sunk, eight to U-boats.

A much-diminished KG 26 returned to Finnmark late in 1944 because they had nowhere else to go. Despite new aircraft, like the Ju188 (shown), they were too weak to pose a serious hazard to a convoy and only with difficulty sank one Liberty Ship, straggling 60nm behind its convoy. (AC)

The ninth, Liberty Ship *Henry Bacon*, was part of RA-64. The convoy scattered during bad winter storms from 18 to 22 February, and *Bacon* was straggling 60nm behind the convoy after its steering gear failed during the final storm.

While the Luftwaffe began transferring back to Finnmark in September 1944, not until February 1945 did they become operational. Forty-eight Ju 88s had been sent searching for JW-64 on 7 February, but failed to find it. On 10 February, 32 torpedo-bomber Ju 88s attacked the convoy but, unlike the Golden Comb attack on PQ-18, all torpedoes missed and five of the attacking aircraft failed to return. This was enough to discourage further attacks on JW-64.

However, RA-64 was soon to pass through the same waters, and KG 26 went after it on 22 February. This raid comprised 19 Ju 88s and Ju-188s (a more advanced version of the Ju 88). While flying to RA-64, they spotted the straggling *Henry Bacon*, and attacked it. It proved a difficult target. The lone freighter's 20mm and 5in antiaircraft guns downed five aircraft and damaged four others. High seas and the ship's gunnery detonated several of the torpedoes launched against it. Eventually, it was hit by a torpedo, fatally wounding it.

Its steadfast defence aborted the Luftwaffe attack on the convoy. Given the damage inflicted by one Liberty Ship, it is likely the Luftwaffe would have fared far worse against a convoy of 33 heavily armed merchantmen protected by an escort carrier. *Henry Bacon* was the last Allied ship sunk by Luftwaffe aircraft, and the last attack on an Arctic convoy by the Luftwaffe.

AFTERMATH AND ANALYSIS

The battle over the Arctic convoys raged from August 1941 until May 1945; 46 months. How necessary were they? Churchill's insistence on them may have been his most important strategic decision of World War II since nearly one-quarter of the Soviet tanks present at the December 1941 Battle for Moscow were provided by Britain. Unloaded at Arkhangelsk, they were rushed by rail to the Soviet capital and, given the near-run nature of the Nazi defeat, it is hard to see how the Soviets could have held Moscow without them.

Until mid-1942, when Soviet factories moved east from Ukraine and western Russia before the Axis overran their original locations reopened, weapons shipped through Murmansk and Arkhangelsk remained critical to keeping the Soviets fighting. Even in 1943, they remained important. Russia won the summer 1943 Battle of Kursk when Arctic convoys were suspended but it could have been more easily and decisively won had the convoys been running and the resources they could have brought been available to outfit the Red Army. Only by 1945 had Arctic convoys fallen into the category of 'nice to have'.

The Arctic run held the reputation as being the deadliest and most miserable of all convoys. The physical misery of the run was never exceeded and the hazards of the sea due to storms and ice were never greater elsewhere than the Arctic run. Even during the Aleutian campaign, both sides avoided the ice pack to the greatest extent possible. On the Arctic run, however, moving through ice was occasionally embraced.

Survival immersed in its frigid water was measured in minutes rather than the hours of the North Atlantic, or days in the tropical Pacific. Combine that with the primitive living conditions at the Russian end of the voyage and the hostility of Soviet officials towards the mariners assisting the Soviets and you have good reasons for men to wish to avoid it.

The run's reputation for combat danger contributed to its dread, yet this occurred largely during just one year, 1942. Of the 104 Allied merchant ships and 18 warships sunk during the Arctic run, 79 merchantmen and 12 warships were lost in 1942. This was over three-quarters of the merchant vessels lost during the length of the campaign. Remove 1942 and the danger of the Arctic run drops significantly, the risk of being sunk roughly equal to that risk on the North Atlantic run.

The presence of the Luftwaffe in force made the difference in 1942. The Luftwaffe was committed to the campaign in March 1942, when the bomber units of Luftflotte 5 began flying operational missions and it remained until November 1942, when those aircraft departed for the Mediterranean. It was most seriously engaged for just five months, from May through September.

During the period the Luftwaffe was present, the Allies lost 70 of the 79 ships sunk in 1942. In the months of the most intense Luftwaffe activity, 69 ships. Not all Allied ships lost during the months of Luftwaffe involvement however were sunk by aircraft or activities related to Luftwaffe activities (such as ships sunk by air-dropped mines). Thirty-four, approximately half, were sunk by aircraft alone, and nine ships U-boats put under were previously crippled by airstrikes. These losses demonstrate the influence of air power on the battle. Of the remaining Allied losses one was sunk by a German destroyer, five lost to misadventure running through their own minefield and U-boats alone sank the rest.

Yet air power was not invincible, even without other aircraft to oppose bombers. Early convoy losses were due to inadequate antiaircraft defences and both the escorts and merchant vessels in these convoys lacked sufficient or heavy enough antiaircraft guns.

The Tribal-class destroyers escorting convoys were optimized for combat against U-boats and surface warships. As built, they had a main battery of eight 4.7in guns, the most powerful of any pre-war British destroyer, but they had almost no light antiaircraft guns and the main battery could not elevate high enough to provide effective antiaircraft defence. These ships were eventually modified to increase their antiaircraft battery.

Similarly, the corvettes, ASW trawlers and minesweepers which provided close escort were excellent for protection against U-boats, but had weak antiaircraft defences. Meanwhile, vessels with superior antiaircraft capabilities, such as the Hunt-class destroyer built with six dual-purpose 4in guns and a quadruple 2-pdr, lacked the endurance necessary to reach Russia with sufficient fuel reserves for combat.

Furthermore, the Royal Navy adjusted to the Luftwaffe's presence. They added RFA oilers, permitting the short-legged Hunts to accompany convoys by refuelling at sea, and they

The Tribal-class destroyers, of which HMS *Afridi* was one, were the pride of the pre-war Royal Navy. Frequently used to escort Arctic convoys, their antiaircraft battery was inadequate as their main-battery 4.7in guns performed poorly in an antiaircraft role. (AC)

added auxiliary antiaircraft cruisers to each convoy. Over time they increased the light and medium antiaircraft batteries of both merchant ships and warships, and wartime construction freighters, especially those built during and after 1942, had formidable antiaircraft batteries. Liberty Ships typically carried at least one 5in dual-purpose antiaircraft gun, often a second 3in antiaircraft gun, with multiple 40mm and 20mm mounted as well.

The effectiveness of a single ship with a well-equipped antiaircraft battery should be emphasized. *Wainwright* single-handedly broke up one torpedo attack on PQ-17. *Scylla* and *Ulster Queen* scattered an attack on *Avenger* by 20 Ju 88 torpedo bombers during PQ-18, downing 11. Later in the war, when KG 26 returned to Norway, the guns of a single Liberty Ship brought down five of 19 enemy aircraft attacking it before succumbing. The problem in 1942 was that the antiaircraft resources available in 1945, or even 1943, were unavailable.

While stout antiaircraft fire could even the odds, the real answer lay in opposing aircraft with other aircraft, particularly aircraft capable of finishing off attacking bombers. This, too, the Allies lacked through much of 1942. The Sea Hurricanes Mk I, carried aboard both CAM ships and *Avenger*, were inadequate; being armed with rifle-calibre machine guns they lacked the firepower to reliably knock down bombers, or even the fragile Condors and He 115s.

Worse, they lacked the speed and flight performance to catch multi-engine Luftwaffe aircraft. They could break up a bombing formation attacking a convoy, but they rarely caught or brought down shadowing aircraft. Additionally, the one-shot nature of the tired Hurricats aboard CAM ships meant those guarding convoys were reluctant to use them.

Nevertheless, *Avenger*'s Sea Hurricanes significantly improved convoy defences during PQ-18. The only unambiguously successful aerial attack on PQ-18, the Golden Comb torpedo attack of 13 September, occurred while no fighters were airborne. It also had the advantage of surprise, but subsequent attacks were broken up, since the convoy knew what to expect and how to respond. The more robust Wildcats used in 1944 and 1945 guaranteed future attacks would be unsuccessful when made in numbers the Luftwaffe then had available.

Ultimately, had the Luftwaffe remained in force in Norway, the new escort carriers and antiaircraft capabilities by summer 1943 would have defeated them. Losses would have been greater than in 1945, but only a fraction of that of 1942. That is a great 'what if', however. The Allies never again attempted wartime convoys during the summer months, largely because of their fear of a Luftwaffe which had departed during the winter.

This was especially ironic as summer convoys were safer from U-boats than those run the rest of the year. U-boats were deadliest attacking surfaced at night, when they could attack unseen, and so the unending Arctic summer days significantly reduced U-boat effectiveness.

Only Luftwaffe reconnaissance units saw use against Arctic convoys in 1943 and 1944. With the Luftwaffe largely gone, Allied losses shrank. Yet fear of air attack led to summer suspensions of the Arctic convoys. (AC)

During daylight they were limited to underwater attacks. For this reason Dönitz was unenthusiastic about committing U-boats to attack PQ-17 before it left port. In the Arctic convoys run between May and July 1942, U-boats averaged only one ship sunk per convoy. This was even true for PQ-17 prior to dispersal – the shipping massacre occurred after dispersal.

If anything, PQ-17 underscored British focus on the wrong threat, the Kriegsmarine heavy units, especially *Tirpitz*. Those ships sank no vessels travelling in Arctic convoys and even Kriegsmarine destroyers sank only three cargo vessels making Arctic runs. Britain's focus on cruisers and battleships left them fighting the previous years' war.

Dispersing convoys when attacked by heavy warships made sense in the wide Atlantic during 1939 through mid-1941, where the air threat was minimal, and even the U-boat threat was limited by their small numbers. In the Arctic, within reach of bombers and plentiful U-boats, it produced disaster.

Convoys PQ-16 and PQ-18 both demonstrated the importance of maintaining a tight formation and promptly obeying the convoy commodore's orders. Losses in both were reduced by maintaining tight formations which concentrated antiaircraft fire. This proved critically important in PQ-16, that had insufficient antiaircraft defences. PQ-18 experienced most of its losses among the ships that missed orders to turn when the Golden Comb attack was launched and six of the eight ships hit by torpedoes were in the columns which failed to turn as ordered.

The campaign also demonstrated that Axis success depended more upon Allied failings than Axis competencies. The Luftwaffe rarely achieved high hit rates – even the successful 13 September Golden Comb attack launched over 80 expensive torpedoes, of which only eight scored hits, most due to a British error. Dive bombers frequently managed hit rates of 5 per cent or less: 19 torpedo-bombers attacked *Henry Bacon*, a slow-moving cargo ship, yet achieved only one torpedo hit, and that only after *Bacon*'s steering failed, leaving it unable to evade.

Despite this the Luftwaffe emerged the victor in its campaign against Arctic convoys, not the Allies. PQ-17 forced a suspension of convoys from mid-July through mid-September, and the losses suffered by them and the cancellation of a similar-sized convoy in August deprived Russia of tanks and military vehicles which could have equipped five Soviet tank corps and five mechanized rifle corps, as well as some 500 aircraft, during a critical period of the 1942 Russian campaign.

In 1943 the Allies suspended Arctic convoys after February and sent no more until November. This was due to the perceived risk to convoys during periods with Arctic daylight. Eight convoy cycles were skipped during these months, convoys which could have outfitted nearly two dozen tank corps and two dozen mechanized rifle corps. It was hardly surprising Stalin was displeased.

Some of this may have been due to *Tirpitz*, however an equal or larger reason for concern was fear of Luftwaffe aircraft. Since the Luftwaffe lacked aircraft in sufficient numbers to launch a campaign against Allied shipping in the Arctic between November 1942 and November 1944, the 1943 convoy suspension was largely a dividend provided by the Luftwaffe's Arctic efforts during the previous year. The gain to the Axis cause was great, even in the Luftwaffe's absence, and far greater than the losses incurred during 1942. It was a rare mid-war victory for the Luftwaffe.

Surviving aircraft and ships

There may be only one aircraft that participated in defending or attacking Arctic convoys, or the peripheral actions, that survives today: Hampden I P1344. Part of 144 Squadron sent to Russia in August and September 1942, it was shot down over Finland while flying to Russia. The wreck was recovered in 1991 and acquired by the RAF Museum at Cosford, England, in 1992. Since then it has been undergoing restoration and, at the time of writing, the fuselage has been restored.

It is extremely unlikely many other aircraft participating in this campaign still survive, Allied or Axis. This is almost certainly true of the aircraft participating during the critical year of 1942. There were a handful of Allied warplanes, but no Axis

The only aircraft known to have participated in the Arctic campaign in 1942 is this Handley Page Hampden. It barely qualifies however, having been shot down entering Russia in August 1942. Its wreck was recovered in Finland in 1991 and brought to Britain. It is currently undergoing restoration at the RAF Museum in Cosford. (The Trustees of the RAF Museum)

bombers used in the campaign in 1942 appear to have survived past the war's end, much less until today.

On the Allied side there is one Mk I Sea Hurricane left, but it served in squadrons that appear not to have been in the Arctic. It is in the Shuttleworth collection at Old Warden Aerodrome in Bedfordshire, England. Fourteen Swordfish still exist, most in Britain, and two of which may be flyable. They are unlikely to have served in the Arctic, however. Similarly, there is only one surviving Fairey Albacore, on display at the Fleet Air Arm Museum, built from bits and pieces of two crashed Albacores.

There is a similar lack of representative Axis aircraft. No complete examples of Fw 200s or BV 138s currently exist, although efforts are being made to restore examples from wrecks. Two He 115s though do still exist. One of these, awaiting restoration at the Sola Flyhistorisk Museum, may have participated in the campaign – it belonged to *Seefernaufklärungsgruppe 906*, which was present in 1942.

There are five surviving He 111s. One belonged to the Spanish Air Force, a second is a CASA-111 built under license in Spain and a third was a transport version commandeered by Army Air Force pilots in France and left in Britain at the end of the war. Two others were combat versions found in Norway and appear to be veterans of the 1940 Norwegian invasion, wrecked during that campaign. (One, operating on a frozen lake, could not be moved before the ice melted in late 1940.)

There are two intact Ju 88s in existence. One is a photo-recon version in the service of the Royal Romanian Air Force during World War II, and is currently on display at the US Air Force Museum at Dayton, Ohio. The second is a fighter version, based in Denmark, and is now in the RAF Museum. Three other partially intact aircraft, all bomber versions, are undergoing restoration, though none served in this campaign. Two are undergoing restoration in Norway (one of which was recovered from the same lake as the He 111), and the third is currently in Germany. While all three saw combat, none served in Norway in 1942 or later.

None of the cargo ships that made the Arctic run still exist, all having been scrapped by the late 1980s. Of the warships on both sides that fought, only one still exists, HMS *Belfast*, berthed in London as a museum ship. It missed the critical year of 1942, undergoing repairs for mine damage, but did participate in later convoys, including being present at the Battle of North Cape, where *Scharnhorst* was sunk.

FURTHER READING

There are many books written about the Arctic convoys, some excellent, others sadly lacking. The problem with most, however good, is that they often fail to put the campaign in its context against the rest of the war. It is easy to get angry at Stalin's unreasonable insistence the convoys sail, regardless of loss, unless you understand the Soviets' desperate need for their cargoes.

Another problem is they tend to focus on one element – merchant shipping, surface warships, U-boats or aircraft – often to the exclusion of the others. As a result I used a very large number of sources, not all of which can be mentioned here. The principal sources used are listed below.

I would like to highlight one in particular. Richard Woodman's *Arctic Convoys 1941–1945* is one of the best one-volume histories of the entire campaign. David Irving's *The Destruction of Convoy PQ-17* is a more controversial book, as much because of Irving's reputation as a

A Hurricat being placed on a training catapult at Speke, Liverpool, where the Merchant Ship Fighter Unit (MSFU) was headquartered. Hurricats played a valuable role guarding Arctic convoys in 1942. (Wikimedia Commons)

Holocaust denier and Nazi apologist as for its idiosyncratic coverage of that battle. Even if Irving treated the senior officer of the escort, Commander J. E. Broome, unfairly, the book is useful.

Two websites proved especially valuable for this book: http://www.convoyweb.org.uk/ has a wealth of information on the convoys, their composition and their losses; https://www.ww2.dk/ is equally valuable about Luftwaffe organization and unit locations.

Two highly entertaining fictional accounts of the campaign can be found in Alistair MacLean's first novel, *HMS Ulysses* and Jan de Hartog's *The Captain*. Conditions on the convoys never got as bad as portrayed in *HMS Ulysses*, but it is an exciting read. De Hartog focuses on deep sea trawlers and tugs, an oft-neglected part of the battle. Both wrote from personal experience.

Blair, Clay, Jr, *Hitler's U-boat War: The Hunters, 1939–1942*, Random House, New York, NY (1992)

Blair, Clay, Jr, *Hitler's U-boat War: The Hunted, 1942–1945*, Random House, New York, NY (1998)

DeZeng, Henry L. IV, *Luftwaffe Airfields 1935–45: Finland*, http://www.ww2.dk/Airfields%20-%20Finland.pdf (Accessed 26 May 2021) (2014)

DeZeng, Henry L. IV, *Luftwaffe Airfields 1935–45: Norway*, http://www.ww2.dk/Airfields%20-%20Norway.pdf (Accessed 26 May 26 2021) (2014)

Fairbanks, Douglas, Jr, *A Hell of a War*, St Martin's Press, New York, NY (1993)

Irving, David, *The Destruction of Convoy PQ-17*, Richardson & Steirman, New York, NY (1987)

Morison, Samuel Eliot, *History of United States Naval Operations in World War II, Volume 1: The Battle of the Atlantic, September 1939–May 1943*, Little, Brown, Boston, Mass. (1946)

Morison, Samuel Eliot, *History of United States Naval Operations in World War II, Volume 10: The Atlantic Battle Won, May 1943–May 1945*, Little, Brown, Boston, Mass. (1956)

Paterson, Lawrence, *Eagles Over the Sea, 1935–42: The History of Luftwaffe Maritime Operations*, Naval Institute Press, Annapolis, MD (2019)

Roskill, S. W., *History of the Second World War, War at Sea, 1939–45: The Period of Balance v. 2*, Her Majesty's Stationary Office, London (1956)

Smith, Peter C., *Arctic Victory: The Story of Convoy PQ-18*, Crécy Books, Bodmin, Cornwall, (1994)

Woodman, Richard, *Arctic Convoys 1941–1945*, Pen & Sword, Barnsley (2007)

INDEX